Modern Analytics Methodologies

Modern Analytics Methodologies

Driving Business Value with Analytics

Michele Chambers
Thomas W. Dinsmore

Associate Publisher and Director of Marketing: Amy Neidlinger
Executive Editor: Jeanne Glasser Levine
Operations Specialist: Jodi Kemper
Cover Designer: Alan Clements
Managing Editor: Kristy Hart
Project Editors: Elaine Wiley, Melissa Schirmer
Copy Editor: Chuck Hutchinson
Proofreader: Jess DeGabriele
Senior Indexer: Cheryl Lenser
Compositor: Nonie Ratcliff
Manufacturing Buyer: Dan Uhrig

ISBN-10: 0-13-349858-1
ISBN-13: 978-0-13-349858-5

Pearson Education LTD.
Pearson Education Australia PTY, Limited.
Pearson Education Singapore, Pte. Ltd.
Pearson Education Asia, Ltd.
Pearson Education Canada, Ltd.
Pearson Educación de Mexico, S.A. de C.V.
Pearson Education—Japan
Pearson Education Malaysia, Pte. Ltd.

Library of Congress Control Number: 2014939827

BUSINESS
HD
38.28
.C444
2015

To my son, Cole, may you help make the world a better place with your math, science, and technology talent. To my mother, who taught me how to be graceful and loving. To my father, who passed his math gene on to me and taught me that there are no limits in life other than those you impose on yourself. To my adopted family, Lisa, Pei Yee, Patrick, Jenny, and Angel, thank you for your love and support.

To the heroes on the front line and those behind the scenes who are working toward eradicating slavery from the face of the earth—may analytic insights help in some small way to achieve this quest in your lifetime.

—Michele

To my wife, Ann; my two sons, Thomas and Michael; my late nephew Jeffrey Thomas Dinsmore; my father, Ralph Boone Dinsmore; and to my grandfather E.W. Egee Jr., who loved new technology.

—Thomas

Contents

Foreword

In the Information Age, those who control the data control the future. I've invested my career in helping develop and bring to market the technologies that help make sense of data. While serving alongside Michele Chambers and Thomas Dinsmore as an executive at Netezza, the firm that invented and launched the world's first data warehouse appliance, I met thousands of business people around the world and heard stories of the challenges they faced turning information into insight. Most of all, I saw an overwhelming demand for practical guidance on how to best take advantage of the wealth of new analytic technologies that were emerging to help organizations make better sense of data. The pace of innovation in analytic technologies makes best practices a moving target, and keeping up with them is a huge challenge. As the executives leading initiatives involving our firm's most advanced analytical capabilities, Michele and Thomas developed deep insights into what it took for firms to fully utilize the most sophisticated analytic technologies in the market. Because of this experience, there are no better people than Michele and Thomas to offer this timely roadmap on *Modern Analytic Methodologies*.

The world around us has become increasingly digital. An ever-expanding collection of digital devices—computers, mobile phones, IPTVs, smart homes, connected appliances, smart hospitals, smart utilities, and more—are creating an explosion of data as we interact with them. This "digital exhaust" produces so much data that yesterday's analytic technologies often fall short. Fortunately, innovation in analytic technologies has accelerated to keep pace with the data deluge. Hadoop, NoSQL, MPP (massively parallel processing) databases, in-memory databases, streaming/CEP (complex event processing) engines, and more—these modern platforms are fully capable of capturing relevant information about nearly every digital interaction occurring anywhere in the world.

Importantly, extracting insights from this growing data volume requires not only new technologies, but also new methodologies. There is no one-size-fits-all approach for analytic architecture, and it follows that business processes and organizational structures must be tailored to support each firm's unique technical approach to data analysis. Because analytics must be linked to business strategy in order to deliver value, best practices are unique to each problem, and each firm's path to success will be unique. What Michele and Thomas offer here is a compelling review of the patterns of success drawn from a diverse set of experiences helping firms address a variety of different business challenges with analytics. This makes *Modern Analytic Methodologies* an invaluable tool in helping you craft your own unique path to success.

Every individual climbs a learning curve over time with respect to his or her ability to leverage data analysis to create success. The uniform truth that I've seen is that individuals that climb this curve the fastest are the ones that win. They are the most highly sought after—and highly compensated—professionals in the world. The payoff is clearly worth the effort. What Michele and Thomas offer in *Modern Analytic Methodologies* is a roadmap for accelerating your journey to take full advantage of the state of the art in analytics.

They have rigorously tested the techniques and best practices they share across a breadth of diverse firms with different business challenges. As a result, they are able to reveal what works and what doesn't. Their real-world experiences have been a crucible for discovering the challenges that analytics professionals face and for evaluating which solutions really work. *Modern Analytic Methodologies* is a battle-tested blueprint for practitioners who want to increase their odds of success.

Brad Terrell
Former VP & General Manager,
Netezza and Big Data Platforms, IBM
Boston, MA

Acknowledgments

Imagine how hard it is to write a book, then quadruple it, and you'll start to feel how much work it takes to write a book. We undertook this project as a labor of love for our field and to give back to others the value of our insights and knowledge. Although a book on technology is never complete because the industry is constantly evolving and morphing, we have finally approached the end for now.

Along the way, we have had the distinct pleasure of collaborating with many thought leaders and who are experts in their own rights. We'd like to thank them for their time, support, and contributions.

Thank you for your contributions:

Sujha Balaji—Philadelphia University

George Matthew—Alteryx

Greta Roberts—Talent Analytics

Les Sztandera—Philadelphia University

Thank you for sharing your experiences:

Dean Abbott—Smarter Remarketer & Abbott Analytics

Thomas Baeck, Ph.D.—Divis Intelligent Solutions

Brandy Baxter—Alteryx

Michael Forhez—CSC

Bob Gabruk—Cognizant

Rayid Ghani—EdgeFlip & University of Chicago

Kevin Kostuik—Charlotte Software Systems

Doug Laney—Gartner

Bob Muenchen—r4stats.org

Tess Nesbitt, Ph.D.—DataSong

Karl Rexer—Rexer Analytics

Greta Roberts—Talent Analytics

George Roumeliotis—Intuit

Thank you for your support:

Thank you, Jeffrey Brown with Accenture, for being a sounding board.

Thank you, Bill Jacobs, Lee Edlefson, Neera Talbert, Rich Kittler, and Derek McCrae Norton, for your valuable review and feedback.

About the Authors

Michele Chambers is the Vice President of Marketing for MemSQL. Prior to this, she served as Chief Strategy Officer and Vice President of Product Management & Marketing for Revolution Analytics, General Manager and Vice President for IBM Big Data Analytics, and General Manager and Vice President for Netezza Analytics. In these roles, Michele has worked with hundreds of customers to help them understand how to use analytics and technology to achieve high-impact business value.

Thomas W. Dinsmore is the Director of Product Management for Revolution Analytics. Previously, he served as an Analytics Solution Architect for IBM Big Data, SAS Consulting, and PricewaterhouseCoopers. Thomas has helped more than 500 enterprises around the world use analytics more effectively. He uniquely combines hands-on skill in predictive analytics with business, organization, and technology experience.

Section I

Why You Need a Unique Analytics Roadmap

1

Principles of Modern Analytics

There was a time, not long ago, when enterprise analytics was simple: You bought software from the leading vendor and installed it on a box. If your needs changed, you bought more software from the same vendor, and installed it on a bigger box. Analytics was a niche field populated by specialists, all of whom used the same software they learned in graduate school. People still believed that a single data warehouse could hold everything worth knowing.

The business cadence was, in retrospect, leisurely: If it took two years to implement a predictive model, well, that was just how things worked. Not that long ago, a big bank ran four campaigns per year to promote its credit card; at the time, executives thought that was an accomplishment.

Well, good-bye to all of that. Digital media is here; so are Web 2.0, mobile, cloud, and Big Data. The volume, velocity, and variety of data are exploding; enterprises are abandoning the ideal of the single data warehouse because it is impossible to stay on top of the tsunami. Diversity rules—we have a plethora of sources, an alphabet soup of platforms, and data everywhere: on premises, hosted by third parties, and in the cloud.

The changing landscape of data brings with it sweeping changes to the field of analytics: new business questions, applications, use cases, techniques, tools, and platforms. Techniques now considered mainstream were exotic five years ago. A single vendor once dominated analytic software; today, there are 851 analytic startups listed in Crunchbase, the leading source of information about startups. Open source software continues to eat the software world: two of the four Leaders in The Gartner Group's most recent Advanced Analytics Magic Quadrant are open source projects, and surveyed analysts prefer open source analytics to the most popular commercial software by more than two to one.

Above all, the cadence of business accelerates exponentially. Yesterday, we ran four campaigns a year; now we can run four campaigns an hour. Nobody can afford to take two years to implement a predictive model; we will be out of business by then.

We can no longer afford the luxury of the blue chip, single-vendor proprietary analytics architecture. In its place, we see enterprises building an open analytics platform based on diverse commercial and open source tools, tied together through open standards. In this new world, each organization must define a unique analytics architecture and roadmap, one that recognizes the complexity of the modern organization and business strategy. This architecture will include many vendors and open source projects because no single vendor can meet all needs.

In this book, we propose an approach based on nine core principles:

- **Deliver Business Value and Impact**—Building and continuously evolving analytics for high-value business impact
- **Focus on the Last Mile**—Deploying analytics into production to attain repeatable, ongoing business value
- **Leverage Kaizen**—Starting small and building on success
- **Accelerate Learning and Execution**—Doing, learning, adapting, and repeating
- **Differentiate Your Analytics**—Exploiting analytics to produce new results
- **Embed Analytics**—Building analytics into business processes

- **Establish Modern Analytics Architecture**—Leveraging commodity hardware and next generation technology to drive out costs
- **Build on Human Factors**—Maximizing and grooming talent
- **Capitalize on Consumerization**—Leveraging choices to innovate

Next, we fully explore each of these principles because they are the foundation upon which Modern Analytics are built.

Deliver Business Value and Impact

Later in the book, we describe how to go about creating a unique analytics roadmap and how to prioritize projects. For now, suffice it to say that one of the principles of Modern Analytics is a focus on analytic projects with potential for game-changing value to your organization. To hold the organization accountable for delivering value, measure your current state to establish a baseline and set initial quantifiable target business objectives and ongoing business objectives. For example, current revenue is $100 million with CAGR 4%. The initial target is to identify 15% net new revenue with an ongoing net new revenue contribution of 10% annually.

Although such a metric can be easy to identify and measure, other metrics can be harder to identify and measure. To discover these potential metrics, identify points where business decisions are typically made. Start by measuring impact at these points. Then work toward establishing metrics that have a direct impact on the business. Whereas in the past, companies typically aspired for either a revenue metric or an operational cost metric but not both, today mature analytic organizations often establish metrics on both sides of the balance sheet. This sends a clear signal to the team that revenue growth has to be accomplished cost efficiently.

Savvy organizations identify potential analytic opportunities by thinking outside the box. Typically, the hardest, most entrenched problems in an industry or company have been around so long that people start to think about them as hard-and-fast constraints for their business. However, often, the barriers that existed in the past that made them impossible to solve no longer exist. Unleashing the bottleneck typically results in massive business value creation. Analytic-driven organizations dare to think outside the box and identify some of the most challenging problems facing their industry or business. When that is done, they work toward identifying how they solve or reduce the problem through innovative data- and technology-driven approaches. This is usually accomplished with a clean sheet brainstorming approach and imagining that all the resources needed to solve the problem exist. After ideas are vetted, the team typically has another brainstorming round to determine how to get everything they need to solve the problem without settling. Instead of using samples or backward validation[1] to estimate a solution, the team will identify potential new resources—data, symbiotic partnerships, or technology—that will help them achieve their business objectives.

To realize the business value both initially and over an extended period of time, you need to deploy the analytics into production. Before any analytics can be deployed, the results of the analytic model need to be validated for accuracy. Today, that typically occurs in a "sandbox" with a limited subset of the data and in an artificial, non-production environment. It is all too common for an analytic model to meet or exceed business criteria in a sandbox but significantly underperform in a production environment. Be sure to evaluate your analytic models based on the environment that they will be deployed into, not any idealistic environment. Deploy the analytic models into a replicated production environment to fully test the model prior to going live to get a realistic assessment against the target business

---

[1] Also commonly referred to as *backtesting*.

objectives. Where deploying used to be a "post" process after the model was built, deployment is now part of the full life-cycle analytic process. Once all potential technical deployment barriers are identified, obtain legal and/or procedural process validation before the "go-live" launch into production. After an analytic model is deployed, measure the initial business impact and identify quick ways to continuously improve on the results.

Focus on the Last Mile

Today, very few organizations get to the promised land of deploying analytics into production environments to drive game-changing business value for their organization. To get to this end goal, start with the end in mind and work backward. Understand day-to-day issues at every level in the organization by speaking with frontline workers—from strategy through to execution. These domain experts are acutely aware of the issues, problems, and constraints impeding their success. Clearly understand what it will take to achieve success—not how success can be attained. With this understanding, set quantifiable and ambitious goals for your analytics. For example:

- What is the target business value to be obtained?

  A 3% lift in revenue?

  Inventory saving of $10 million annually?

  Total cost savings of $100 million in the first year of deployment?

- What is the expected service level agreement (SLA) for the business?

  Reevaluated credit scores nightly?

  Portfolio evaluation within 5 minutes?

- What is the operational model?

  How does the model get moved into production?

Does this analytic model need to integrate with other business systems? If so, how do the operational processes and decisions change?

Is this analytic model triggered from another business system?

Is this analytic model deployed in one location or multiple locations?

Are there multinational or localized requirements?

What is the frequency of updates to the model?

- What are the key success factors that measure the business impact?

How is success measured?

What constitutes failure?

How long does the team have to achieve success?

- What is the model accuracy?

Is the accuracy "good enough" to realize immediate business value?

How much should the model be improved in what period of time?

Traditionally, one team—quants, statisticians, or data miners—has been responsible for the model creation while a second team—typically IT—has been responsible for the production deployment. Because this often crosses organizational boundaries, there can be long lags and disconnects between the model creation and the model deployment or scoring. The teams must function as if they are one team even if organizational boundaries exist and will persist. A full life-cycle methodology can serve to bring these two teams into alignment if the analytics methodology goes beyond just creating and assessing the initial analytic model to encompass the actual production deployment and ongoing reassessment of the analytic model to achieve the business objectives.

With Modern Analytics, teams focus on delivering results quickly rather than waiting to build the "perfect" analytic model. They do so by starting with Proof-of-Concepts (POCs) or prototypes that may be limited in scope, but help the organization increment toward realizing business value. They quickly mature and harden the POCs or prototypes into a production deployment where the rewards can be systematically reaped.

Leverage Kaizen

Kaizen, the manufacturing movement for continuous improvement, is being adapted into many different disciplines, including analytics. The core tenements of Kaizen are to

- Start small.
- Remove overly complicated work.
- Perform experiments to identify and eliminate waste.

There is an emphasis on delivering value quickly rather than completeness. Testing and learning can make small improvements along the way while working toward the end goals.

This is a marked contrast to the current tendency to spend long development cycles building the "perfect" models. Today, building and deploying analytics are complex, custom projects that cross over multiple functional areas. In this new era, modern analytic teams are removing the ivory tower academic shackles from traditional analytic methodologies to eliminate unnecessary, time-consuming steps from the project cycle. This helps increase agility and responsiveness while incorporating business feedback into the process so results can be improved.

With Kaizen serving as a guiding principle, modern analytic teams build and deploy models immediately and then improve on the models in short burst cycles dovetailing the work of analysts and IT to create a frictionless environment that continuously delivers business value. On the ground, the teams often use hybrid agile or rapid application development methodologies to improve cycle time and reduction in barriers with cross-functional teams.

Accelerate Learning and Execution

Today, modern analytic teams are trying new things—experimenting with new and combined approaches, tools, visualizations, and algorithms to uncover patterns in the growing mass of data. By trying new things, experimenting and transferring lessons from one industry and problem to a completely different industry and problem, modern analytic teams have significantly accelerated their learning and are driving new business value. However, to foster this level of innovation through experimentation, there has to be a culture that tolerates and expects failure as a path to learning and improving.

As an example, as data sizes have increased, modern analytic teams have started shifting away from constrained, statistical-only approaches to predictive and machine-learning approaches that can leverage the power of all of the data. One of the key lessons learned as data has increased is that the underlying tools and infrastructure need to minimize data movement in order to meet business objectives, especially for service-level agreements. Modern analytic teams have quickly realized the transferability of this lesson to various types of analysis and have incorporated these lessons into requirements at the onset.

Today, by industry standards, 60–80% of an analyst's development time is spent doing data preparation or data munging. Another valuable lesson that modern analytic teams have discovered is that the upfront manual data munging should be minimized, and instead, data prep tasks should be automated and/or handled as part of the analytics processing activity. This dovetails with the need for businesses to move at a faster pace to be ahead of the competition. The ability of an organization to learn in as close to real-time as possible is a trend whose momentum will continue to build. The ability to uncover patterns in real-time, act on them almost instantaneously, and continue to discover deeper insights to improve the next cycle is a requirement in the modern business world.

Differentiate Your Analytics

Businesses strive to create competitive differentiation through a combination of products, customer service, and operational processes that are delivered to the market. Analytics can simply support each independent activity by delivering comparable insights as realized by competitors. Or they can be used to highly differentiate your competitive strategy. That could mean being a first mover—the first or on the leading edge of using analytics in your industry—or it could mean distinguishing your analytic approach or the speed at which you deploy your analytics into a production environment.

Many firms look around the marketplace and try to learn from their competitive landscape. However, that copycat approach typically means settling for a secondary position in the market rather than a leading position. Instead, analytic leaders look at other industries and how they're using analytics. They draw analogies between problems from other industries and the problems in their business. They discover how other companies are using analytics to solve their problems. They start to look for new data and approaches outside the four walls of their organization. They forge new symbiotic alliances to obtain data and methods that benefit their organization. They apply the new knowledge to problems in their industry or business. To do this, they look beyond the silo of their own team, department, or location. They look for opportunities to integrate with other data and processes to build an analytic solution with a broader impact for the organization. They remove the constraints they've lived with and find new ways to inspire innovative analytics. They use the full breadth and combination of available analytics—not just what they've always used—to drive game-changing value. They don't just create predictions; they use their predictive model to systematically perform at their best by optimizing the predictive model to prescribe the best course of action. This relentlessly drives the best course of action—day in and day out—to help them achieve their competitive differentiation.

Embed Analytics

On-demand or ad hoc analytics are analytic models that are executed occasionally and provide a "point in time" insight that can be used by a human to inform decisions and take a course of action. While this approach is useful and provides value, it is slowed down by the human interaction. Think about financial traders of years gone by. Traders would run desktop tools on the trading floor to understand complex financial market interdependencies. The tools would produce a "spot"—or instance in time—view of the market, and the trader would use that to inform them as to what to buy or sell. Today, the capital markets are dominated by "algorithmic trading," where a sophisticated program, which embodies a newer generation of the algorithms that were in the desktop tools, automatically makes trades. Eliminating human interaction and embedding analytics into the complex financial market process eliminates friction in the overall system. When the analytic models are built into the process, repeatability and scalability are achieved. This relentless execution drives incalculable business value in the marketplace.

Establish Modern Analytics Architecture

As analytics has matured over the past 20 years, analytic architectures have gone through a substantial transition from standalone desktops to enterprise data warehouses to Big Data platforms such as Hadoop. High-performance computing environments, such as clusters and grids, which were once specialty environments, are becoming mainstream environments for analytics. This has created a hodgepodge hardware and software legacy in data centers across the globe. All of this has occurred while the cost of computing power has dramatically decreased and open source software has gone mainstream.

The paradigm shift underway is a movement toward building lean analytic architectures, as illustrated in Exhibit 1.1, based on simplicity and open standards that leverage commodity hardware and open source software to drive the costs out of the architecture, provide platform scalability, and leverage the latest innovation. This innovation supports the execution of thousands of computationally and data-intensive predictive models in production deployments by large user bases with differing analytic and service-level requirements. Building, managing, and supporting the ecosystems required to deliver on these requirements means incorporating many different hardware and software products—both open source and proprietary. Even within a single vendor, products oftentimes don't integrate seamlessly due to generational changes in software and acquisitions. Lean analytic architectures use a proprietary hardware and software solution when the solution provides a unique value but insist that the solution has open interfaces that make it readily integrated to other solutions.

The streamlining reduces the complex administration and maintenance costs while creating efficiencies for analyzing and deriving insights from the data.

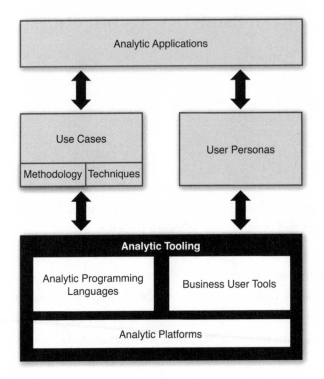

Exhibit 1.1 Modern Analytics Framework

Build on Human Factors

Flashy news headlines and hype have organizations believing that there are elusive individuals, known as data scientists, who embody the consummate triumvirate of deep expertise in computer science (software engineering, programming languages, and database skills), analytics (statistics, data mining, predictive analytics, simulation, optimization, and visualization skills), and domain expertise (industry, functional, or process expertise). Although there are some (actually precious few) individuals with this combination of skills, there is a growing realization that the elusive data scientist is actually a team of individuals who work closely together to fulfill the objective embodied in the data scientist role. These teams usually include a handful of multidisciplinary data scientists who are part of the senior leadership in the team. To analytic-mature organizations, this is readily apparent and mirrors their experience in growing into an analytic-mature organization.

As the field of analytics has matured, the breadth and scope of analytics in organizations have increased. There is no longer just one type of role that builds, uses, and understands analytics in an enterprise. Instead, there are multiple roles or personas, each with different skills and responsibilities. Analytic-savvy organizations build on the human capital in the organization and understand what personas they have and what personas they need to achieve their business objectives. Various roles and personas contribute to the business differently, and all the personas are typically critical to achieving the business objectives. When there is a gap in skills, these organizations invest to bring the individuals or team up to speed. Analytic personas value new knowledge, and that's a key component to keeping the scarce resources committed to your organization. By broadening and elevating the interests, awareness, and skills of your analytic professionals, you'll keep the team engaged and innovating for your organization.

Capitalize on Consumerization

Consumerization of information technology continues to gain momentum in the marketplace. Consumerization today takes several forms, including "app stores," crowdsourcing, and BYO (bring your own).

B2B app stores and markets have analytic apps emerging. Some of these apps are very narrow, discrete use cases, such as a credit scoring formula, whereas other apps are more comprehensive end-to-end use cases, such as multichannel marketing attribution. Although none of these may be a complete 100% fit, they can provide a starting point to speed up time to insight and drive down costs.

Crowdsourcing is a type of outsourcing through which an enterprise solicits contributions from an online community to perform a specific task. Crowdsourcing analytic models or algorithms provide access and leverage of outside expertise that would be difficult or impossible to access at an economical rate.

The "bring your own" era of self-service is well underway with analytic professionals who are demanding to use their favorite tools, data sources, and models rather than the standard information technology or mandated equivalents. Although information technology typically seeks to standardize and consolidate vendors and tools for cost and ease of support, analytic professionals typically value other considerations, such as user interface ease of use, flexibility to tailor via programming interfaces, and breadth of analytic models. Out of this tension has arisen the self-service approach to bringing your own:

- Data (BYOD)
- Tools (BYOT)
- Models (BYOM)

BYOD—bring your own data—is a way for organizations to combine their noncompetitive data to discover patterns and derive insights with new rich data sources. BYOT—bring your own tools—is a way to mix and match open source and proprietary technology tools to address specific service-level agreement requirements. BYOM— bring your own models—is a way to leverage app stores and crowdsourcing to derive value.

Summary

The principles of Modern Analytics chart the path toward analytic transformation and maturity in an organization. On the ground, these newly emerging principles of Modern Analytics are reshaping analytics from the bottom up in organizations. Today's business leaders are reshaping the next era of business—Business 3.0—from the top down driving automated, fact-based decisions, execution, and results.

To power your competitive differentiation, you must have a unique analytics roadmap to supercharge your business strategy to make the transformation from the Information Age into the next evolving age of faster changing business competition where epiphanies and agility to use those epiphanies to shift your business to the next level are key to thriving.

This book starts with the revolutionary stories to inspire you and which you can learn from and apply to your industry and business. We then transition into a framework that will allow you to identify opportunities throughout your organization for applying Modern Analytics. Some of these have never been attempted before; therefore, you may be breaking new ground. Don't let this discourage you; the risk takers reap the highest rewards. Even if your initial attempts fail, learn from them so that when you use the technology and approaches for other applications, you learn from your mistakes. Some of your ideas for applications may not be completely new ideas but may be innovative in their approach, which may produce better results for your organization. This framework will allow you to systematically identify a wide variety of opportunities that align with your specific business strategies and objectives to uncover hidden value in your business that is lying dormant waiting to be discovered.

In the following chapters, you learn more about organizations that are transforming their businesses with analytics in this new age and how you can create a unique analytics roadmap for your organization.

2

Business 3.0 Is Here Now

When I first meet people, I often ask, "Who were your heroes growing up and why?" I have found that in this simple question, you learn a lot about a person. You learn about their core values—in other words, what makes them tick. Their response helps you to understand their framework or outlook on life and the mark they want to leave as their legacy.

My heroes were John Wayne, Helen Keller, and Amelia Earhart. John Wayne's characters were always bigger than life for me, and they stood up for their values. The combination of swagger and humanity that characterized his roles struck just the right balance of machismo and compassion. Helen Keller represented achievement despite adversity. This woman forged a path that is easy to forget today but which I believe was the turning point that changed and continues to change our outlook on disabilities. Lastly, Amelia Earhart represented a willingness to take risks, learn from her mistakes, and take on bigger challenges.

We are fortunate enough to be living in a period of time when there is constant change. I am also fortunate enough to be in a field (technology) where change is the norm and those who embrace change are forging a new world order. Although you could argue that this change is leaving some people and some parts of the world behind, I would argue that a rising tide lifts all boats.

In this new age, there are unsung heroes—the modern day revolutionaries who are creating a tide swell of change. These revolutionaries are the risk takers who have bet their careers or their business on a science that early on failed to meet the hype but later proved so instrumental that many of their legacies can't be told because they are trade secrets. These diehards held fast to their beliefs that this new and evolving science would make the world a better place, despite all the adversity they faced in successfully deploying it in their business. Today, as Big Data and Modern Analytics appear to be the darling children of technology and business, it's easy to forget the revolutionary heroes who took those risks to help this point in time unfold.

In this book, you'll learn more about some of their stories and how they're pushing their businesses to new heights. This book isn't about using technology to make incremental changes in your business. This book is about how you can use technology to create disruption in your business and industry. This book describes how you can apply technology to areas of your business that have remained untapped by the potential of this technology. We share tales about revolutionaries who have taken unique approaches in combining technology to achieve success. We also share experiences about those who are creating the next wave of applications—very intelligent applications that, although they aren't quite as intelligent as the human mind, certainly have advantages over the capacity of the human mind to process complexity.

To place context around this paradigm shift, let's digress a bit into recent business and technology history.

Some of you may be old enough to remember the first wave of automating business processes (if not, look up the history of mainframes and IBM applications starting in the early 1950s) such as order processing, fulfillment, and so on, and how that wave of technology enabled businesses to create sustainable competitive differentiation for several decades. The initial competitive differentiation came from either being early to market as one of the "haves"—those who had the resources to afford the technology to automate their process—or being one of the "have nots." However, over time, companies realized that as more businesses automated, they lost their competitive differentiation with only automation.

Then in 1993, Michael Hammer and James Champy disrupted the market by introducing the "reengineering" concept in *Reengineering the Corporation*.[1] Even though we had decades of automation, businesses were still holding onto many of their legacy business processes (now automated) and people who were oftentimes redundant. Hammer and Champy outlined a process for streamlining businesses and reducing waste and inefficiency. This period was hallmarked by a period of painful workforce reduction in order to cut costs to differentiate business value.

Just four years later, building on the work of Hammer and Champy, Michael Treacy and Fred Wiersema in *The Discipline of Market Leaders*[2] introduced three fundamental value disciplines that characterize all business:

1. Customer Intimacy

2. Product Innovation

3. Operational Excellence

Treacy and Wiersema outlined how companies use a combination of these disciplines to create unique competitive differentiation—usually choosing a "major" and "minor" and being equal to the competitive landscape on the third strategy.

In today's world, the opportunity at hand is to create the next generation of automation. But this isn't your father's notion of automation. No, no, it's a new more intelligent automation. It's a way to imbue a whole new generation of applications that are smarter and to connect the dots similar to the way the human brain does.

---

[1] Michael Hammer and James Champy, *Reengineering the Corporation* (New York: HarperCollins, 1993).

[2] Michael Treacy and Fred Wiersema, *The Discipline of Market Leaders* (New York: Perseus Books, 1997).

While for the foreseeable future we won't have applications that are smarter than the most knowledgeable, seasoned experts, there will be a new generation of applications that use the combination of knowledge from our best and brightest minds, combined with oodles of data—much more than the human mind can digest—to rapidly synthesize complex considerations and identify patterns to predict or prescribe the best course of action, very much the way our most seasoned experts—research scientists, doctors, CEOs, and so on—lead their organizations today. Unlike the previous period of automation, the next generation of applications—Modern Big Data Analytic applications—will be tightly aligned with the major and minor business strategies. By tightly aligning with the business strategy and being proactive rather than reactive, businesses will be able to "pulse," or move faster and smarter in a way that is unique to their industry and business.

The struggle for many organizations, even those that use the new tools and approaches, is to identify new and innovative applications that will help them realize the promise of the game-changing value. The best organizations look outside their industry and try to extrapolate how an innovative application fits their industry and business. Although this practice is often successful, it's a hit-and-miss proposition that leaves executives lacking a comprehensive approach to move their entire organization to the next level—a level where they've created a sustainable competitive differentiation by creating Modern Big Data Analytics barriers throughout their organization that underpin their business strategies and create a relentless execution model that makes it darn near impossible for the competition to topple.

Just as the heroes who embarked on new adventures—Amelia Earhart, Christopher Columbus, Neil Armstrong, Steve Jobs, and many others—you too are about to embark on an adventure that has the potential to change your world. Embrace it and make it your legacy.

3

Why You Need a Unique
Analytics Roadmap

Overview

Although consultants publicly shout that every business is unique, they privately whisper that businesses are all the same. How can that be? Well, at a surface level, businesses appear, especially within an industry, to produce comparable products and use the same processes. So why is it then that some businesses succeed, whereas others stall and some simply fail? It's not what they do that creates the uniqueness, it's how they do it. The "what" describes their business strategy and the "how"—or the operational execution of their business strategy—creates their value proposition in the market. Those that distinguish their execution create a unique value proposition that forms sustainable competitive differentiation as described by Michael Porter in the timeless business classic *Competitive Strategy: Techniques for Analyzing Industries and Competitors*.[1]

Enterprises seek to create unique advantage through disciplined execution by an organization of people. However, the global marketplace is moving faster and is more complex than any other time in history. How can enterprises create a sustainable advantage when people are increasingly becoming overwhelmed with data and decisions? By

[1] Michael Porter, *Competitive Strategy: Techniques for Analyzing Industries and Competitors* (New York: Free Press, 1998).

powering their unique business strategy with a unique analytics strategy tailored to help them achieve their business goals, by leveraging the data, and by moving to faster execution of fact-based decisions.

To create a unique analytics strategy, an enterprise must leverage a variety of assets, expertise, and techniques to create a unique analytics roadmap that will propel it into the analytics fast lane where analytics supercharges the operational execution of the enterprise's unique business strategy. To create a unique analytics roadmap, enterprises need to think outside the box and determine how to exploit analytics for their competitive advantage. Today, the application of analytics is in its infancy. To unlock the full potential of analytics for an enterprise requires a systematic discovery approach that marries the business with the technology assets and capabilities. In this discovery, consider how each of these capabilities applies:

- **Business area**—How can we apply analytics to a new business area or problem?
- **Data**—What data can we invent or enrich our analytical insights?
- **Approach**—How can we employ a combination of analytical approaches in an innovative way to discover new patterns and value?
- **Precision**—What additional value would we realize if we could identify individuals (people, transaction, or resources) rather than groups?
- **Algorithms**—Can we create or use new groundbreaking mathematical or scientific approaches that give us an advantage?
- **Embedding**—How can we systemize our insights by inserting analytics into operational processes?
- **Speed**—How can we accelerate our pace of business to stay ahead of the competition?

Next, we discuss each of these capabilities further.

Business Area

The first generation of analytics was most successful in a few business areas: customer and marketing analytics, supply chain optimization, risk, and fraud. Today, with the second generation of more powerful analytics that are available, opportunities to apply analytics exist in every facet of an enterprise—sales, marketing, operations, distribution, customer support, finance, HR, risk, procurement, compliance, asset management, and so on. This means that every segment of your organization can benefit from the insights of analytics. The areas of your business that are key to your core value proposition—the "major" and "minor" fundamental strategies—will benefit the most from custom-tailored analytics that underpin your unique operational execution of your business strategy. For the other business areas, off-the-shelf analytic solutions (to the extent that they exist in the marketplace) can be used to drive comparable competitive value. This combination provides an organization with a unique analytics roadmap that is a combination of custom-developed and purchased analytic solutions that underpin its unique business strategy.

Data

The analytics strategy needs to help the enterprise go beyond its own four walls—to utilize new and emerging data sources that aren't locked up inside the enterprise's own four walls in legacy transactional systems—to help it enrich its ability to drive new, high-value insights that simultaneously drive the top line of business cost efficiently throughout the enterprise, not just in one area of the business. The question isn't "How do I leverage the data I have?" but "What would I like to know, and how could I use that insight to help add value to my organization?" Leveraging new and powerful data sources is part of the story, but there are also opportunities to connect the dots to derive information that isn't readily available. By using this combination of rich new data, enterprises can gain significant business value.

Approach

You often hear the term *data science* bantered about and used to mislabel first generation analytic practitioners rather than the new generation of multidisciplinary scientists who can curl up with data,[2] dissect problems, and use scientific approaches to employ a unique combination of analytical techniques to discover new patterns and value. These data scientists don't view a problem as simply a statistical problem or an operations research problem, but instead have the ability to understand the business problem and apply the right combination of analytic techniques—for example, data mining plus simulation plus optimization—to solve the problem and drive huge business value for organizations. Because it is difficult to find all these skills in any individual, it is more common to find a data science team—with a mix of skills, experiences, and perspectives from mathematics, statistics, science, engineering, operations research, computer science, and business—that brainstorms and collaborates closely to produce a unique approach to solving the problem. Teams such as these exist not only at Internet businesses, such as Google and Facebook, but also at large banks, retailers, and pharmaceutical companies.

Precision

Precision—or fine-grained control—is about driving insights down to individuals rather than groups or aggregated data. As an example, shifting from traditional demographic segments to segments of one manifests marketing precision. For instance, precision involves understanding that my buying behavior is significantly different from

---

[2] Thank you, Dean Abbott, for the great term!

that of my neighbor even though our household income and age range are almost identical. My buying behavior is driven by the fact that I'm a single mother of a teen and my neighbors are grandparents to two adorable toddlers.

More generally, precision is about understanding unique characteristics that motivate individualized behavior in people, processes, or events. By understanding the individualized behavior, you can predict the future behavior more precisely.

Algorithms

Algorithms are the combination of steps to calculate a result for a specific purpose. There are algorithms for just about any problem you can imagine—from the simplest of problems, such as average, to sophisticated, highly specialized algorithms, such as self-organizing neural networks that automatically extract and analyze chemical shift differences.

In industries that have been using analytics for quite some time, using new innovative and often specialized algorithms can help drive the incremental value needed to edge out the competition. This is most evident in the financial services industry where algorithmic trading relies on the increasing sophistication of highly specialized algorithmic techniques.

Embedding

Embedding analytics into automated production processes is a technique used to continuously execute based on analytical insights to drive the highest value for the organization. Typically, embedding is achieved through a continuous closed loop process that reevaluates and improves the model or through a self-learning and adaptive technique. This relentless operational execution through a continuous learning and improvement process is often regarded as sophisticated to implement, but it is the technique that drives continuous and relentless value for organizations.

Speed

Although each of these approaches is disruptive, speed allows you to consistently outpace the competition. When you use analytic speed to drive insights, you create an agile and frictionless environment that allows your organization to relentlessly outperform on your core value proposition.

Summary

In summary, a unique analytics roadmap exploits the right combination of these approaches to drive game-changing results with the highest business value for the organization:

- Applying analytics to new business areas and problems
- Leveraging new data sources to enrich insights
- Using innovative approaches to discover and exploit hidden patterns
- Creating or employing cutting-edge algorithms to gain advantage
- Embedding analytics into production and operational processes to relentlessly and continuously improve the business processes
- Accelerating the pace of analytic insights to outperform the competition

Section II

The Analytics Roadmap

4

Analytics Can Supercharge Your Business Strategy

Overview

Analytics is one of the tools that can help you create a unique value proposition. Yes, analytics gives you the power to describe what has happened within your industry and business. But more importantly, analytics gives you the ability to discover and automate what you can *do* to realize revenues and operational savings that directly tie to your specific business strategies. Analytics can give you the power to make complicated trade-off decisions even when the objectives conflict with each other. Analytics can help you make better decisions even when you don't have a lot of data or the data you have isn't reliable. Analytics can help surface so-called known unknowns that point out voids, or whitespace in patterns of your data, which help surface and highlight opportunities that are often overlooked.

In a nutshell, analytics gives you the ability to grow top-line revenues cost efficiently. This is a simple but very powerful statement. To give you a glimmer into the world of possibilities, imagine that you can

- Introduce a new product and start generating profits in half the time it currently takes

- Repeatedly hire people with the right raw talent and other factors to be successful in a specific role, dramatically increasing business performance and reducing employee churn and training costs

- Determine likely competitors' moves before they make them and proactively mitigate their moves by introducing your own strategic move to take advantage of market opportunities

- Create individual incentives for all your customers that allow you to maximize profitability and loyalty

- Anticipate costly production-down situations and eliminate or minimize their impact

- Consistently introduce new products for which there is latent, unmet demand in the market

- Continually set pricing strategies for micro-niches that maximize profitability over time

- Discover the whitespace for your product in targeted geographies and the appropriate tactics to deploy to dispel your competitors and win those customers

As you can see, the possibilities are limitless. The organizations that understand how to produce these types of results systematically—those with high analytic maturity—are clear market winners. By extracting value from better forward-looking models that influence their business strategies and underpin their operational execution, these top-performing analytic-driven organizations are reaping the rewards of first-mover advantage and establishing technology barriers that make it increasingly difficult for competitors to win against.

Case Studies

Several prestigious research studies, including "New Path to Value" published by MIT Sloan School of Management in October 2010,[1] show that top-performing organizations view and use data to drive analytic insights throughout their organization to create differentiation. This research was followed up by another Sloan School of Management study, "Analytics: The Widening Divide," published in November 2011[2] that demonstrated how analytic-driven organizations employ analytics to quickly create significant differentiation from their competitors while managing risk much more effectively.

Take, for example, Google, which won the online advertising world through analytics. Or Walmart, which won the big box retail wars through supply chain optimization. Or Capital One, which invented and won the subprime credit market through analytic segmentation. And the financial markets have been irrevocably disrupted through algorithmic trading.

Many of these analytic successes exist in the marketplace today, but the details of how they achieved their success are often considered trade secrets. Many of these stories aren't publicly disclosed or are disclosed at highly technical conferences where other scientists can learn from the analytic approaches, but the business lesson and value aren't clearly communicated. It's no wonder that businesses continue to apply analytics to the same old problems using the same old analytic techniques because it seems as though those are the only problems on which analytics can be applied.

However, you're about to discover a breakthrough innovative application of analytics that can inspire you and your team. These examples are about analytics applied to new business areas and problems, using innovative approaches often with new data, to drive

---

[1] http://sloanreview.mit.edu/reports/analytics-the-new-path-to-value/.

[2] http://sloanreview.mit.edu/reports/analytics-advantage/.

analytic insight to a new level of precision throughout the business. These stories are about visionaries, leaders, and modern-day heroes who are charting a new course—a course that connects dots across the business and around the globe to drive new analytical insights and action for their organization.

DataSong Discovers Customer Interaction Insights

DataSong,[3] formerly known as Upstream, is a cloud-based marketing software-as-a-service (SaaS) provider that does multichannel marketing attribution phenomenally well and helps its customers, such as Williams-Sonoma and Neiman Marcus, answer the elusive marketing question:

> "Half the money I spend on advertising is wasted; the trouble is I don't know which half."
>
> —*Attributed to John Wanamaker*

This was certainly true in the early 1900s when Wanamaker stated it, but does it apply today? We certainly have many more marketing tools and channels today. And marketing today is a data-rich environment. But do we measure marketing spend and return rigorously? Are we spending our marketing budgets effectively today?

Most companies today use traditional techniques such as marketing mix models or volumetric models for determining marketing attribution, a technique to approximate which marketing tactic should receive credit for a sale. Marketing mix modeling typically uses multivariate statistical analysis time series data from sales and marketing to estimate the impact of marketing tactics on sales. Volumetric models are typically survey based and attempt to understand purchasing behavior. Both techniques use aggregated information to perform attribution of marketing spend to sales conversion.

---

[3] http://www.datasong.com.

DataSong helps its retail customers identify the most profitable marketing channels for each of the retailers' individual customers. DataSong does this by understanding the marketing spend in each marketing channel (that is, direct mail, email, mobile, online, search, advertising, and so on) and how that directly links to sales across all the sales channels (such as call center, in-store, online, mobile, and so on). Understanding how marketing spend (such as catalog) and combinations of marketing spend (such as catalog plus email) impact conversion into sales is key to understanding how to

- Utilize marketing dollars to achieve sales objectives
- Optimize the use of marketing budgets

Using large volumes of transactional sales data—including every impression served, every website click, every email delivered and clicked through, every catalog sent, and every postcard sent—DataSong customers use their marketing budgets much more efficiently, generate more demand, and realize more sales.

DataSong developed analytic models by applying techniques used in biostatistics and medical research—survival analysis—that are not commonly used in marketing. It used these techniques because it recognized that the impact of the marketing tactics has a time-dependent outcome or decay; in other words, after a prospective buyer receives a specific marketing treatment (such as a catalog), the potential for a purchase decreases over time. The longer it takes for the customer to react to the offer, the less likely he or she is to purchase. When a sale does occur, the analytic model uses the sales conversion to allocate "credit" to the various marketing channels.

Tess Nesbitt, Ph.D., is a fellow and senior data scientist at DataSong and a modern-day pioneer who describes the DataSong multichannel marketing attribution:

> Our methodology focuses and puts each customer under the microscope which allows us to build models at the customer

level. This is a very different approach than a marketing mix volumetric approach that uses aggregated information. By modeling at the customer level, you develop a deeper understanding of incremental effects that helps customers realize huge financial rewards. If you want to send the right message to the right person at the right time, you need to understand individualized incremental effects. By understanding the relationship of timing between marketing messages and sales conversion, we know when to send specific market tactics to increase the chance of purchase. Our models sift through a growing number of data sources with terabytes of data, processing billions of rows with 500+ attributes, to find patterns and differences between customers. Let's take a catalog or an email as an example. We can learn which type of customer is going to be more impacted by which specific marketing treatments. This helps us to do better targeting. Timing in sales and marketing is critical. By knowing when to send the right message, we significantly increase their chance of purchase.

After DataSong has done the time-dependent attribution of sales to specific marketing treatments, it can use this insight to fuel many other marketing insights including

- Optimizing marketing mix across various sales channels
- Reallocating marketing spend to maximize sales and return on investment (ROI)
- Targeting specific customers (for example, the most profitable) with specific marketing treatments (that is, those most likely to trigger purchase) at the right time

The data-driven, time-to-event survival analysis framework that DataSong uses handles competing risks to establish a target objective and distribute revenue at the individual customer level. The large volume of data takes into account internally generated data (purchasing history, clickstream, web impressions), customer-driven information (store location, seasonal factors), as well as special case information (branded search, economic conditions).

In building these models, Nesbitt and the team at DataSong analyze customers for a year or more. According to Nesbitt,

> We analyze customer actions for a year or more. If a customer makes a purchase today, I can see how long ago they clicked on the email and I can see how long ago they got that catalog. I can see how long ago they direct loaded to the website. We're carefully tracking all that information. If they got a catalog a month ago, but then they did all this other activity between receiving the catalog and purchasing, then the activity they did most recent to the purchase [is] more likely to have a bigger impact on compelling the purchase. We'll attribute more credit—if you got a pair of shoes for $100, we'll attribute more credit to the fact that maybe you direct loaded, five days before the purchase, and less credit to [the] catalog you received 30 days before. Marketing attribution is really a combination of the timing relative to your purchase, as well as the amplitude of the effect, of purchase amount. As my boss likes to say, "Usually when people direct load, they have their credit card right on the dashboard." So those variables get more credit, their amplitude, their effect is stronger. We include both online and offline marketing activities, including integrated brand messaging, affiliate sites, TV and magazine advertising along with non-marketing activities in our efforts to identify true incremental sales. There are a lot of cases where marketing activities are getting 100% of the credit for sales but in reality there are external drivers also—like Christmas, annual birthday gifts, and economic and seasonal factors. By inspecting the data at an individual level, we develop a familiarity with the customer that is uncommon in analytic models. That familiarity allows us to correctly attribute variance across everything that's causing somebody to purchase.

Customers often perform "test and control" experiments as well as backtest[4] the DataSong models against its own in-house marketing mix models. The DataSong models have held their own, delivering huge savings and incremental revenues to DataSong clients. For example, one customer saved $250,000 on a single marketing campaign. Another multichannel retailer realized that marketing was responsible only for approximately 50% of overall sales—both offline and online. The other half is attributed to the customers' buying habits and store trade area. This allowed the retailer to redeploy a $5 million marketing budget to another more effective channel within three months. Yet another retailer tested the sophisticated survival model against an industry-leading model and realized 14% lift in response rate and $270,000 in new revenue from a single marketing campaign. This retailer also used the model to determine which customers were likely to purchase without receiving a catalog. That allowed the marketing circulation to be reallocated—stretching the marketing spend—to new channels, which increased the total net new revenue from the campaign. The unique approach by DataSong increases sales revenue and maximizes marketing spend while targeting customers much more precisely.

Talent Analytics Elevates Workforce Performance

In the era of talent wars, Talent Analytics is a predictive analytics software company focused on using advanced analytics to predict top and bottom performers, predict employee churn, and predict top-performing employee performance, including hard-to-find-and-keep data scientists. As the founder and chief executive officer of Talent Analytics, Greta Roberts is passionate about using analytics to deliver employee performance results, not HR results. Talent Analytics software combines raw talent metrics with line of business performance

---

[4] In backtesting, a new predictive model is used against historical data to compare how the new model results compared with the current model.

data sets (sales, performance reviews, how long someone has worked there, anything the business wants to model). As Roberts describes,

> The most mature area of analytics is customer analytics. At the heart of both customer and talent analytics are people. Companies collect a huge amount of data about their employees, everything from their start date, to their compensation, to the resumé that the person submitted originally, to all of the performance reviews plus all of the other content, every e-mail the person ever sent, and so forth—just huge quantities of data. However, they are not generating value out of the talent information they collect. Much of the so-called "talent analytics" done in HR is limited to reporting historical information—a good start but does not pave the way for predicting future performance. Our goal is to help businesses leverage existing employee data to understand how employee raw talent drives business results that can be an extraordinary advantage for a business.

In the United States, there are 160 million workers, and the typical business payroll is 40% or more of revenue. The emerging area of talent analytics is focused on making that cost more productive in modern ways—by creating high-performance teams with a focus on execution and by reducing attrition. By analyzing the data, you can put people in roles where the probability of their being successful increases. Talent Analytics software measures innate characteristics, or "raw talent," to discover what it takes to be successful in the role at the organization. Roberts explains, "We look at past performance of employees to create predictive models which takes into account innate characteristics of individuals to create a 'profile' for what it takes to be successful in specific jobs at a company. For example, is there a kind of person that tends to survive and thrive in this role for 18 months, with an engagement score of 'X,' who also meets their sales goals at least 100% for four quarters?"

As an example, one customer of Talent Analytics, a very large financial services organization, has an outsourced call center that sells and services its own portfolio of products as well as those of third parties. It hires 30,000 call center representatives a year and had a 64% attrition rate. The call center management team clearly understood they had a hiring and attrition problem. They had made several attempts to remedy the attrition problems without success. After digging into the problem further, they realized they had a lot of data about the call center—talk time, call quality score, customer service scores, and much more—but weren't leveraging it to gain any insight about their call center employees. Roberts describes the process:

> They would hire call center representatives in class sizes of 80 people. Day 1 these new hires would begin 12 weeks of training because they had to complete their Series Seven Exam before they would actually start—before they could put them on live customer calls. It is a difficult exam. This class of 80 new hires would begin leaving their role almost immediately. This training is difficult and requires a lot of study time. When the new hires would complete the training the firm would give them one opportunity to pass the exam. If they failed, they would fire them; if they passed the new hire would begin working. New hires were paid for 12 weeks with no return to the business. ROI for this firm was 13 new hires that made it through 12 weeks of training. Then work would begin. Call centers are an interesting use case as almost everything is scripted for everyone in exactly the same way, and yet some employees are successful and some are not. Each employee uses the same script (in fact, call center representatives are typically discouraged from being creative). Managers train representatives to keep the talk time down, stick to the script. And yet some people are successful and some people aren't. It is a fabulous control group to understand, "How come this

group is extraordinarily successful using the same script as these people that aren't using the same script?"

Talent Analytics used their unique approach of scouring the data to find a pattern to define what traits a top performing call center representative possesses. It included characteristics such as not being very friendly, being excited about learning new things, and being internally motivated by the contests that were offered. Using the criteria, they selected the top performers. For those 800 people, they measured their Talent Analytics scores based on a questionnaire that develops a raw talent profile for each individual. Next they looked at the top performing criteria—the actual data on their call quality scores and their call links, and how long they've been there—for 800 people. Then they optimized the predictive models for those five criteria and those variables—a factor analysis of many variables—that they had been given to score the successful reps so that they could align them with the predictive models. They then applied the model to a validation data set. This helped test the predictive models and demonstrated whether or not the raw talent scores can act as an independent variable when hiring could predict line of business results such as talk time.

> The results were astonishing. Top call center representations had a strong set of raw talent characteristics. It was simple at that point to upload our models—created in R—into our Advisor software's benchmarking module. New candidates completed an online questionnaire to calculate their raw talent scores and compared them to ideal. Attrition dropped by a little over 30% in just eight months, for a saving of several millions of dollars annually.

Not only did this approach save millions by reducing attrition, but by hiring the right personnel—the right talent for the job—the company increased the success rate per employee, which drove more revenue. Plus, the reduced hiring was a huge time and cost savings for the organization. "Time after time, our customers realize that analytics can really help to figure out how they can help the businesses perform better, and that directly affects financial performance," states Roberts.

Beiersdorf Leverages Avant Garde Analytics for Product Innovation

Beiersdorf, a long-time leading international cosmetic and healthcare company famous for brands such as Nivea, Eucerin, La Prairie, and others, started using cutting-edge advanced analytics almost a decade ago to expedite its innovative product development. In consumer products companies such as Beiersdorf, being responsive to shifting market needs is critical to business performance and financial results.

As a company with a long history of innovation, Beiersdorf had a huge database with more than 100 years' worth of results from experiments pertinent to the industry. This rich repository was used as the basis to develop new formulations to make entry into new market niches that helped expand the product portfolio and market reach. The endeavor started with the need to develop a new product to meet latent demand in a new target market with a natural product. The traditional approach used in the industry is to experiment with new product formulations—typically variants of known formulations—to create a new stable product that meets the specified criteria such as absorption, fragrance, and other desired characteristics for the target market. It takes time to identify the potential new product formulations, create them, and then determine if they are stable over an extended time period. Using an unconventional approach called *fuzzy logic*,[5] the company used the historical data on experiments

---

[5] Fuzzy logic is a type of analytic reasoning that uses linguistics to understand information and determine the probability of the information being true or false.

to derive rules that were validated by the seasoned team of product development scientists. Using these rules, the company created a predictive model to eliminate experiments that would result in unstable formulations and to identify formulations that would likely produce highly stable formulations. After the set of stable formulations was determined, the stable formulations were "evolved" using a technique called *evolutionary strategy*.[6] All of the potential formulations, including the newly derived formulations, were evaluated to create a recommendation for the best candidate formulations to meet several competing objectives, such as best fit to the latent market demand, minimization of production cost, and several others. This time-saving approach allowed the product development scientists to zero in on the potential natural product formulations that would meet the market requirements as well as the quality objectives for a stable formulation. After the process and model were fully vetted by the scientists, the model was embedded into the product development process and applications for regular use by the team.

Beiersdorf modernized its innovative product development process by applying advanced analytic techniques to slash product development life cycles while discovering new products that meet specific market criteria. The result is that it can quickly launch successful products into the market, giving the company a competitive advantage and continuing its revenue and market growth.

The software that underpins this success story is now commercially available via Divis (http://www.divis-gmbh.de).

Air Liquide Drops Operational Costs

Air Liquide is the world's largest supplier of industrial and medical gases. In the United States, the company's industrial pipeline in

---

[6] Evolutionary strategy is an optimization technique based on naturally occurring adaptation and evolution techniques to mutate and create new potential solutions.

the Gulf states traverses 1,800 miles, carrying two gases—oxygen and nitrogen—from production plants to more than 8,000 customers nationwide. Energy deregulation in the late 1990s forced Air Liquide to transform its business for efficiency because energy is the largest cost driver in producing the two gases. Air Liquide set a goal to shave 4% of its operational costs but blew that away by achieving an 8% ongoing operational saving as a result of fully integrating advanced analytics into its operational systems.

Air Liquide embarked on a journey through multiple projects and phases to eek out cost and inefficiencies in its complex supply chain. Through the use of a combination of powerful advanced analytic techniques, including ant systems and genetic algorithms, Air Liquide was able to develop a comprehensive solution that simultaneously optimized its production schedules and distribution. This powerful multi-objective optimizer uses production planning information combined with customer demand, both spot and forecasted energy prices along with a seven-day weather forecast to optimize the production of the two gases at the U.S.-based production facilities. At the time this innovative optimizer was put into production, it represented one of the largest and most successful industrial applications of ant systems anywhere in the world, saving the company approximately $1.5 million per quarter at a single plant due to the improved efficiency. This was the result of being able to consistently capitalize on market lows for energy prices and ongoing optimization of production schedules at near real-time speed based on changing conditions. A subsequent project integrated another predictive model with its back-office systems to model variable cost drivers and automatically recommend optimal hydraulic and transportation solutions that minimize cost and reallocate valuable resources for the right activities. This effort resulted in further cost savings in the range of $300 to $750 per hour while allowing Air Liquide to automatically adjust to evolving real-world conditions automatically. While continuing to refine its initial efforts, Air Liquide has enjoyed more than $5 million in savings as a result of its vision and pioneering efforts.

Software similar to this success story is now commercially available via Charlotte Software Systems

(http://charlottesoftwaresystems.com).

Thrilling Customers While Driving Higher Profits

Dean Abbott,[7] an internationally recognized data mining and predictive analytics expert, has worked on advanced analytics projects for more than two decades in both defense and commercial industries across a wide variety of applications. Currently, Abbot is the Chief Data Scientist and Cofounder of Smarter Remarketer, a customer-centric marketing intelligence platform that enables retailers to create highly advanced, precisely targeted segments of visitors. His pragmatic, business value-based approach to real-world problems makes him unique in an industry often dominated by ivory tower experts.

Abbott helped a small, curious, and innovative internal team at a computer hardware and devices services center create a secret weapon back in 2010 that, according to Abbott, is still "too critical of a strategic asset for the company to put into the public exactly what they are doing. This very small team at the electronic industry field service company turned out to be rock stars in profitability for the company with the results of a very innovative set of models."

The company recognized it had a problem with field service calls because its service technicians often didn't have the right part on hand to repair the problem on the initial appointment. This resulted in delays and inefficiencies for customers, time-consuming and costly reworks, plus increasing customer dissatisfaction.

To prevent the truck from having to return to the depot for the part, the internal information technology team transcribed call center records and started trying to correlate key words from inbound calls with initial service call dispatches that didn't have the right part on the

---

[7] See Abbott Analytics at http://www.abbottanalytics.com/data-mining-consulting-services-about.php.

truck. The team started pulling up key words using SQL on service calls that needed a part to successfully complete the repair to see if there was any relation between the key words from the customer calls that came into the call center and a part being needed for the repair. The results of the initial text analytics were interesting but not yet insightful enough to systematically rely on.

Abbott assisted the team in pulling the results from the key word analysis—really text analytics—into a predictive model based on decision trees.[8] Initially, the predictive results were poor. After further data mining and munging,[9] the team realized the decision tree approach had two shortcomings. Decision trees perform best when there is a lot of known information (or fairly dense information). The team had been using the individual ticket that had relatively little (or sparse) information and no historical information about similar tickets. Additionally, there weren't a lot of key words for the decision tree to base the decision on.

According to Abbott, the team started brainstorming, and that's when the innovation occurred:

> We started brainstorming and thinking, okay, what's really happening with these service tickets? We started thinking about what's going on historically with the tickets, and we knew a lot of information from the ticket; things like what kind of device had the problem, what's the area of the device that's affected, what's the error code that shoots up for that part of the device, what region is the device located in and who is the customer[?] And, of course, we knew the key words associated with whatever device was used. The innovation turned

[8] A decision tree is a type of analysis that uses a tree-like graph to illustrate possible choices between various options and their probability.

[9] The term *data munging*, or simply *munging*, is commonly used to refer to the tedious task of data cleansing and transforming to allow the data to be used in analytics.

out to be that the team said okay, let's look at what happens historically with these service tickets.

The team started using the service repair history from the field to gather pertinent descriptive statistics for each ticket. They used statistics such as

- For each failure code (for example, 40 or 41), what percentage of the time last year was that failure code associated with a repair that needed a part?
- For each key word, what percentage of the time was this key word involved in a part being needed to complete the repair?

Why was it important to have statistics about the repairs? Because the statistics could be used to weight the choices in the decision tree, thus improving the accuracy of the decision significantly. As Abbott describes,

> What started using the statistics to make more "dents" on the actual key word; instead of a key word being a flag—a 1 or a 0—and leaving it all up to the decision tree to make inferences from the millions of tickets, now there is a more information rich variable that has a percentage associated with that key word. And it wasn't just the key words, when they looked at the resolutions, they could also look and see what was the reason code associated with the repair, and how did the key words and the ticket relate to the resulting repair disposition?

> The innovation really was rolling up historical data into the currently observed categorical variables that were used in the decision tree. That's not innovation for people who live in the space, but that rolled up data turned out to be the pivotal piece of data to unlock the insight which brought about the value that is still considered trade secret.

This technique is commonly used in analytics: Instead of placing the single variable into a predictive model, you capture a summary or other statistics about that variable and add it into the model. For example, in fraud analytics, looking at transactional purchases, you could use the billing address ZIP code to see if that's predictive. But usually what's more predictive in that situation is to associate another measurable characteristic related to that ZIP code. You could look at the historical fraud rate for all the ZIP codes before the outcome because the current outcome is known.

Abbott summarizes,

Once the team used the statistics along with the key word, the model started "popping" or making decisions very obvious. We realized that we needed a part to be used about 90% of the time for the ROI to be worthwhile. That meant that many of the terminal or end nodes in the tree were useless since they were for values in the middle like 30% or 50%. The second innovation that occurred was that we said, okay, a single decision tree is probably not going to get us there and it didn't really get us there. It didn't give us enough cases with the 90% plus of parts used rate in order for the model to be useful. So, the second innovation was don't just build one tree; build lots of trees. This was a kind of ensemble[10] approach. But instead of averaging all the thousands of trees as is typically done with ensembles, we just cherry picked terminal nodes from the thousands of trees. So we built trees with tens of thousands of terminal nodes. And of those, there were at least hundreds of terminal nodes that had a high proportion of a part we needed.

---

[10] Ensemble models are an approach in which multiple models are combined to improve the predictive capability of the model. For a good introduction to ensemble models, see *Ensemble Methods in Data Mining: Improving Accuracy Through Combining Predictions* by Giovanni Seni, John Elder, and Robert Grossman (Morgan and Claypool Publishers, 2010).

After the trees were built, the team recognized that there was quite a bit of overlap in the trees because there were synonyms and surrogates in the key words. This had the effect of creating separate trees for similar information but the information was not quite exactly the same either. This effectively gave the team a set of rules or conditions that could be used together to create a hierarchy of decisions.

Abbott elaborates further,

> There was a lot of overlap between the trees. For the good terminal nodes, there could be surrogates and synonyms and a lot of overlap. However, it's not like these hundreds of terminal nodes were providing hundreds of disparate decisions where we could predict 90% plus parts would be used. But the trees weren't perfectly correlated either, so it gave us this envelope of "or" conditions—let's say if a particular key word was in the rule for particular types of customers, historically, and the failure codes resulted in a part being needed, that would give you one rate. But if the key word results in a part being needed that was in a different bucket—you know, instead of greater than a third of the time of this key word because it's just greater than 20[%] of the time with this key word—that will give it different conflicts. These "or" conditions allow the model to fire sequentially from highest percentage of first used down to lowest, and it created an ever increasing number of new hits with the new service calls coming in so that was always relevant.

The combination of the unique approach—text mining, descriptive statistics, and ensemble learning—to build a predictive model gave them a highly reliable and accurate model that continues to increase profitability and deliver fantastic results. The model is accessed via the company's call center application and allows the company to place parts on repair trucks proactively so that service technicians can satisfy calls on the first attempt. This gives the company a competitive edge and has allowed it to increase customer loyalty, reduce reworks, and utilize spare parts inventory efficiently.

P&G Simulates Policy Changes to Slash Inventory

Procter & Gamble (P&G) is one of the world's most formidable consumer products companies with more than 300 brands, including household names such as Pampers, Tide, Pantene, Bounty, Crest, Olay, and many others. More than 5 billion consumers in over 160 countries use P&G products. In the late 1990s, P&G realized that it had two major problems that were negatively impacting business: (1) excess inventory in its supply chain estimated to be $3.8 billion, and (2) too many out-of-stock occurrences in retail locations, with 11% of the top items being out of stock at any point in time. With the renowned P&G discipline, the company set a goal to reduce inventory by a billion dollars in three years without worsening the out-of-stock situation. Within two years, P&G had reduced inventory by 50% but was hitting a brick wall with further reductions and was seeking new breakthrough solutions.

One of the leaders on the P&G team was a fan of the book, *At Home in the Universe: The Search for Laws of Self-Organization and Complexity* by Stuart Kauffman (Oxford University Press, 1996). In this book, Kauffman shares his insights on complexity science for laymen and goes on to explain how simple systems that grow over a period of time often reach a tipping point where the complexity forces the system to self-organize into a new system with a life and order of its own. The P&G leader reached out to Kauffman, by then the cofounder of BiosGroup, to see whether he could help P&G with a breakthrough solution to its complex supply chain problem.

The BiosGroup team studied the problem, the progress that had been made up till that point, and accepted the P&G challenge to identify another 50% of inventory cost savings. To understand the complex supply chain at P&G, BiosGroup used *agent-based modeling*[11] to create an adaptive simulation of the supply chain—initially for a subset of SKUs—and then building out from there after the simulation was validated. The simulation modeled the entire supply chain—plants, store distribution centers, stores, trucks—along with customer demand, purchasing history, promotions, and inventory. When the model accurately reflected the supply chain, various conditions such as changes in order and shipping policies, manufacturing practices, and promotions could be tested and evaluated to determine the impact on cycle time, inventory, and out-of-stock condition through the simulation. The model was executed thousands of times with different configurations and conditions. With each execution of the simulation, the agents "learn" the best behavior and use that knowledge to evolve and further adapt in the subsequent iteration of the simulation. As the system evolved over time, it became clear that the relatively linear, sequence-based model of the supply chain was being supplanted by a highly linked or networked economy where goods ebbed and flowed smoothly between the plant, distribution centers, retailers, and ultimately to customers.

As the simulation continued to evolve, P&G started field-testing the insights derived from the simulation and started seeing progress toward its goal of reducing inventory without adversely affecting out-of-stock condition at the retailers. With that initial success, P&G embarked on the journey to transform its supply chain into a consumer supply network resulting in $900 million in inventory saving initially, $300 million in ongoing annual inventory reduction, and a 75% reduction of stock outs. One of the key discoveries was that a restrictive order size quantity—which was done to reduce transportation costs by mandating order quantities that would fill up a truck—was creating havoc in the supply chain. This "local" optimization—reducing

---

[11] Agent-based modeling is a simulation technique used to understand complex systems as a group of many independent, simpler agents acting autonomously whose interactions result in a new complex system.

transportation costs—had a trickle-down impact throughout the complex network: Customers held orders back in order to meet the requirement that could trigger stock outs, and when the shipment arrived, they had to store excess inventory in crowded stock rooms, which made it hard or impossible to locate product in their stores where there were stock outs. This was a counterintuitive finding for the P&G team, and the simulation allowed team members to see and experience the implication of their policy decision firsthand. By modifying the possible order size quantity by as little as 5%, the entire system flowed much more smoothly. Ultimately, P&G changed its order size policy to encompass flexibility up to 30%.

The insights and policy shifts that started in the early 2000s from this breakthrough series of projects led to the early pioneering implementation of radio-frequency identification (RFID) and electronic product codes (EPC) to capitalize on real-time demand signals from retailers. P&G remains on the forefront in its industry by using advanced analytics throughout its business.

Summary

Each of these stories illustrated different points about data, approach, algorithm technique, implementation, precision, and speed to drive value for the respective organizations. Exhibit 4.1 summarizes each of the stories along these dimensions for reference.

Exhibit 4.1 Summary of Analytic Case Studies

	Business Area/ Problem	Data	Approach	Precision	Algorithms	Embedding	Speed
Air Liquide	**Product Operations** • Multiobjective pipeline optimization	**Customer data** • Demand forecast • Customer location **Production data** • Production plans • Production output • Product quality • Inventory **Pipeline data** • Equipment data • Equipment location **Energy pricing data** • Daily/spot pricing • Seven-day pricing forecast **Weather data** • Seven-day weather forecasts **Accounting data** • Production costs • Delivery costs	• Ant colony optimization • Genetic programming • Multi-objective optimization	• Hourly production schedules	• Ant systems • Genetic algorithms	• Production pipeline system • Back-office applications	Near real-time

Business Area/Problem	Data	Approach	Precision	Algorithms	Embedding	Speed
Beiersdorf **Product Development** • Product innovation analytics	**Product data** • Formulations/recipes • Ingredients/components **Quality data** • Quality targets **Experimental data** • History of experiments	• Fuzzy modeling • Evolution strategies • Machine learning • Nonlinear optimization	• Formulation	• Fuzzy logic • Support vector machines • Linear models	• Product development process	Batch
DataSong **Marketing** • Multichannel marketing attribution • Micro-targeting • Marketing mix optimization	**Retailer data** • Purchasing transactional history • Advertising impressions • Customer & retail locations • Clickstream • Direct mail • Advertising placements **Third-party data** • Acxiom • Experian • Exact Target • Responsys • Omniture • Core Metrics • Dotomi	• Survival analysis	• Individual customer	• Logistic regression	• Production Scoring	Batch

	Business Area/Problem	Data	Approach	Precision	Algorithms	Embedding	Speed
Dean Abbott	**Field Service** • Field service repair parts prediction	**Call center data** • Calling history **Field service data** • Service tickets • Parts inventory	• Text mining • Ensemble learning	• Individual service ticket	• Descriptive statistics • Decision trees	• Production scoring • Embedded into call center application	Batch
Talent Analytics	**Human Resources** • Talent analytics	**HR data** • Employee information **Call center data** • Calling history	• Predictive analytics	• Individual employee or candidate	• Multivariate factor analysis	• Production scoring and benchmarking	Batch
P&G	**Supply Chain** • Consumer supply network simulation	**Plant data** • Orders • Shipments • Inventory • Transportation plans and costs **Distribution center data** • Shipments • Transportation plans and costs **Retail data** • Purchases • Inventory • Promotions	• Agent-based modeling	• Per SKU	• Agent-based modeling	• Demand planning • Transportation planning	Near real-time

As these stories illustrate, top-performing organizations are using analytics to supercharge their businesses. They are doing so by influencing their strategic moves as well as operationalizing their execution through systematic embedding of analytics throughout their businesses to move toward an analytic-driven, frictionless environment.

5

Building Your Analytics Roadmap

Overview

An *analytics roadmap* is key to creating a unified, holistic vision over time to align analytic projects with the overarching business strategy and goals. The roadmap evolves over time and serves as a communication vehicle for the organization. Although you can create a technology roadmap in many ways, this chapter provides an approach that we've used with analytics and had success with in the past.

Step 1: Identify Key Business Objectives

Your analytics roadmap starts with the end in mind; that is, you need to clearly understand what your business objectives are so that your analytic applications help your business achieve its end goals. Whether you use the fundamental value disciplines described in previous chapters or you have your own principles that guide your roadmap, you need to start with that in mind.

In this section, we use the fundamental value disciplines as the guiding lights to build a sample roadmap that we use throughout the book.

Example: Key Business Objectives

The example we use is from work done in conjunction with a mining consultancy for a mining company whose primary discipline is operational excellence and its secondary discipline is customer intimacy. Three key business objectives were to

- Improve efficiencies throughout operational processes
- Minimize waste
- Increase agility in the market

Step 2: Define Your Value Chain

After you define the key business objectives, the next step is to define the value chain for the organization. There are many methods for defining value chains as originally defined by Michael Porter in *Competitive Advantage: Creating and Sustaining Superior Performance.*[1] In a nutshell, the value chain identifies the primary or core activities of a business separately from the support activities. This provides a handy framework to focus in on how analytics can add value to an organization. Core activities are areas of the business where analytics can and should be used to create competitive differentiation through custom analytic solutions. Support activities are secondary priority areas for analytics and where analytics simply provides table stakes. Support areas are typically well served by packaged analytic solutions if they are available because packaged applications provide "me too" capabilities rather than high-value analytic solutions.

---

[1] Michael E. Porter, *Competitive Advantage: Creating and Sustaining Superior Performance* (New York: Simon and Schuster, 1985).

Example: Value Chain for Mining Industry

In the value chain example for the mining industry (see Exhibit 5.1), the core activities focus on identification, mining, sales and marketing, and the delivery of the minerals, and the ancillary activities are a combination of business services and support.

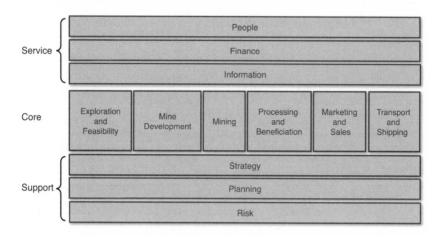

Exhibit 5.1 Mining Industry Value Chain

When the key discipline, key business objectives, and the value chain are combined, the path to a roadmap starts to unfold around analytics that can create competitive differentiation in the areas of core activities. The analytics need to be highly tailored to the business processes in these areas, whereas the analytics in the service and support areas can be more commodity or off-the-shelf packaged analytic solutions to the extent that they exist in the marketplace.

When a high-level value chain is identified, the next step is to decompose or drill down in the value chain until there are finite value chain steps. Typically, three levels are sufficient.

Example: Drill Down of Core Activities in the Mining Industry Value Chain

In this mining industry core activity decomposition, level one consists of Project Startup, Mining and Processing, and Logistics and Sales (see Exhibit 5.2). Level 2 consists of Exploration and Feasibility through Transport and Shipping. Level 3 is decomposed with enough specificity to begin the brainstorming of specific analytic solutions to address the key business objectives for the value chain step.

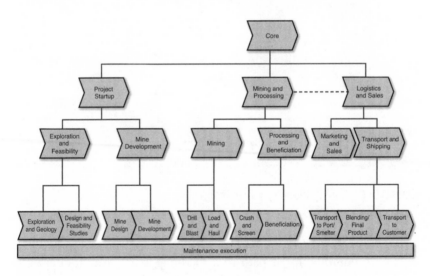

Exhibit 5.2   Decomposed Value Chain

Step 3: Brainstorm Analytic Solution Opportunities

The next step is to brainstorm potential analytic solutions per each value chain step. Within each value chain step, a variety of potential analytic solutions are possible, including strategic, managerial, operational, customer-facing, and scientific. Each of these types of analytic solutions addresses a different time horizon, turnaround time, and deployment.

The following is a description of each of the types of analytic applications:

- **Strategic**

  Definition: These infrequently used analytic solutions typically provide high value and are operationalized through an offline decision or process. They tend to have an outlook over an extended time frame (for example, one to three years).

  Example: In strategic network design, the entire distribution network is analyzed and optimized to reduce capital asset expenditures, lower operational costs, and anticipate network expansion to reach new markets and demand. Network design is reassessed periodically (for example, annually or every three years) to determine what, if any, changes need to be undertaken. This evaluation doesn't occur more frequently because the changes have a cascading impact on the entire supply chain.

- **Managerial**

  Definition: These less frequently used analytic solutions typically provide value through midterm planning. The implementation of this type of analytics is often executed through semi- or fully-automated processes. Managerial analytics tends to have a shorter time frame outlook (such as three months to one year).

  Example: Demand planning takes into account various demand signals, including customer purchasing history, inventory levels, lead times, upcoming promotions, and much more, to predict purchase demand and cascade anticipated demand into production processes and throughout the supply chain.

- **Operational**

  Definition: These types of analytics are embedded into the front line processes for an organization and are executed as part of the day-to-day operations. Operational analytics ranges from real-time (now) to short-time horizons (today or this week).

Example: Real-time ad targeting uses streaming, real-time web and mobile data combined with historical purchases and other behavioral information to display targeted advertisements on websites instantaneously.

- **Customer-Facing**

  Definition: These are analytics that typically provide value by providing insights about customers. These also tend to range from real-time to short-time horizons.

  Example: Personalized healthcare analytics uses personal biometrics along with huge repositories of knowledge about diseases and anonymized patient information to help consumers understand the impact of their day-to-day actions on their immediate and long-term health.

- **Scientific**

  Definition: These types of analytics add new knowledge—typically in the form of new intellectual property—to an organization. The frequency may be periodic (every year) or occasional (once every several years).

  Example: Drug discovery analytics uses information about existing drugs and diseases to determine new applications of existing drugs. Additionally, analytics is used to identify potential new derivative drugs that can address diseases at a molecular level.

To brainstorm various analytic solutions for each value chain step, review how analytics is used to address various business issues. This is best accomplished by understanding the types of problems various analytic techniques can help solve. Analytic techniques include

1. **Descriptive analytics**—These types of analytics describe what has happened in the past.

- What happened?
- Why did it happen?

2. **Predictive analytics**—These types of analytics use data from the past to anticipate the future by identifying valuable connections and insights from the past data.

- What's likely to happen?
- When will it likely happen?
- Why will it happen?
- What happens if these trends continue?
- What's the relationship between specific characteristics and likely outcomes?

3. **Simulation**—These types of analytics repeatedly model random events to understand the likelihood of various outcomes.

- What else could happen?
- If we changed these things, what would happen?

4. **Prescriptive analytics**—These types of analytics evaluate many (if not all) of the potential scenarios to determine the best or a set of best possible scenarios to achieve the goal(s) given various constraints.

- What is the best/worst that can happen?
- What are the trade-offs between best outcomes?
- What is the best plan to execute?

To get ideas flowing, start with probing questions for each value chain step. Examples of probing questions include

- What if you could...?
- Is there something in your business that you wished you knew today rather than in the future?

- What would be a beneficial early warning signal? What data would constitute the early warning signal?
- Where do you think there are hidden patterns that could benefit your company?
- Where would it benefit your organization to make the best decision possible?
- Where would it be beneficial to understand trade-offs in making the best possible decision?
- Where would it be beneficial to narrow in on a set or portfolio of best outcomes?
- Where would it be beneficial to help to understand various scenarios?
- Where would it benefit you to know how much is needed and where?
- Where would it benefit you to know what will happen next?
- Where would it benefit you to know what is the best that can happen?
- What could you learn by connecting new data and systems? What data would be needed? What systems need to be integrated? What are the benefits of connecting those dots via systems?
- How could you drive new revenue streams?
- How could you increase profitability?
- How could you foster innovation?
- What are the right investments to make to outpace the competition?
- How do you know when to do...?

- How can you drive higher profitable customer loyalty?
- How can you find more customers like your most profitable customers?
- Who is the most likely to...?
- Is there something about your customers that you'd like to know that would help you drive new sales opportunities or better service your customers?
- What is the optimal way to do...?
- What if you could predict when...?

The brainstorming can be facilitated by any of the well-known brainstorming techniques such as

- Nominal group
- Directed brainstorming
- Guided brainstorming
- Mind mapping
- Group passing
- Question brainstorming

Use the technique or techniques that work best with the team that is participating in the brainstorming.

Example: Identified Analytic Solutions

Exhibit 5.3 shows the results of a brainstorming session for two value chain steps. In the example, we just used a portion of the analytic application types (that is, strategic, managerial, and operational) to illustrate that you can scope down the brainstorming to a portion of the potential applications, or you can use the full scope.

	Mining	Processing and Beneficiation
Strategic	• Strategic Integrated Planning Optimization	
Managerial	• Tactical Integrated Planning Optimization • Mine Development Planning Optimization • Pit Design Optimization • Geostatistical Modeling • Disaster Recovery Planning Optimization • Operations Training Cockpit • Load and Haulage Optimization • Mine Effectiveness Optimization • Mobile Equipment Fleet Optimization	• Mill Optimization • Crush and Screen Optimization • Beneficiation Process Optimization
Operational	• Operational Scheduling Optimization • Geostatistical Ore Body Model Reconciliation Optimization • Load and Haulage Scheduling Optimization	

Exhibit 5.3 Analytic Solutions

Step 4: Describe Analytic Solution Opportunities

After the brainstorming has exhausted potential analytic solutions, the next step is to elaborate on each of the ideas. This is a brief summary of the potential solution with key elements that explain the idea simply and concisely. Key elements include

- **Description**—A summary explanation of the potential analytic solution.
- **Issues addressed**—A list of business issues addressed. Through experience, this part of the summary is best framed as a set of questions that will be addressed by the potential analytic solution.
- **Data sources**—Initial thoughts on data and/or data sources required for the solution.

- **Analytic techniques**—Initial thoughts on the analytic techniques to be employed in the solution.

- **Impact on value chain**—An initial summary of the potential qualitative and quantitative business impact on the value chain.

Example: Analytic Solution Descriptions

As you start to flesh out the initial ideas, some natural consolidation or elimination may occur, as illustrated in Exhibit 5.4 and Exhibit 5.5.

Strategic Integrated Planning Optimization

- **Type of Analytic Application**
  - Strategic

- **Description**
  - An optimization of the use of existing assets to maximize value. This includes optimization across mine planning, mobile equipment beneficiation, transport, and the associated maintenances.

- **Issues Addressed**
  - Where should we locate stockpiles across the globe to minimize costs and be able to respond quickly to customer demands?
  - If we add double-track rail, does that investment create significant dividends in the global demand chain network over laying down single track?
  - What is the best design for our demand chain today? Five years from now?

- What is the best rail track design to a new mine?

- What do we need to build/buy to solve for the 999 MTPA?

- **Data Sources**

  - Mine plans, equipment sensors, MES quality, transportation plan, equipment maintenance plans, and cost accounting

- **Analytics Techniques**

  - Predictive Analytics

  - Optimization—Multi-objective optimization

- **Impact on Value Chain**

  - Decrease capital assets expenditure through better use of existing assets and predict when new assets will be needed so we can purchase when it's most cost-effective.

- **Value Discipline Alignment**

  - Primary: Operational Excellence

  - Secondary: n/a

Exhibit 5.4   Strategic Analytic Solution Description

Mobile Equipment Fleet Optimization

- **Type of Analytic Application**

  - Managerial

- **Description**

  - An optimization of capital expenditures, utilization, and assignment of mobile equipment

- **Issues Addressed**

  - Which equipment should go where across the company to optimize the supply chain while achieving production and quality targets?

- What other mine should we deploy drilling equipment to when a mine shuts down?
- What other mine should we redeploy our blasting equipment to when the iron ore body is different than expected in a mine?
- What trucks should we divert to which mine when a stockpile quality is lower than expected?
- Which equipment should go where in this mine to optimize the demand chain while achieving production and quality targets?
- Where should we deploy drilling equipment within the mine when there is a shutdown?
- How should blasting equipment get redeployed within the mine when the iron ore body is different than expected?

- **Data Sources**
  - Equipment sensors, facility locations, production plans, transportation plan, and MES quality information

- **Analytics Techniques**
  - Predictive Analytics
  - Optimization—Multi-objective optimization

- **Impact on Value Chain**
  - Decrease costs
  - Increase yields
  - Increase production agility
  - Increase equipment utilization

- **Value Discipline Alignment**
  - Primary: Operational Excellence
  - Secondary: n/a

Exhibit 5.5 Managerial Analytic Solution Description

For reference with the mining example, we were able to identify 45 individual potential analytic solutions across 22 value chain steps with varying degrees of business impact on the value chain.

Step 5: Create Decision Model

Most organizations will be able to identify more potential analytic solutions than time or budget will permit. Therefore, organizations need to agree on a manner to prioritize the solutions to create a roadmap. A simple decision model helps gain consensus across the organization and with stakeholders while taking into account various decision criteria.

Example: Evaluation Criteria

To establish a simple decision model, establish evaluation criteria that can be used to assess the potential analytic solutions. Evaluation criteria can be strictly quantitative, but often it is satisfactory to have a combination of both qualitative and quantitative criteria. Each criterion should be weighted relative to the other scoring criteria to establish importance of the criterion in the overall decision (see Exhibit 5.6).

Exhibit 5.6   Evaluation Criteria

Evaluation Criteria	Description of Evaluation Criteria	Weight
Business Value Fit	Relative business value of solving the problem	35%
Industry Need Fit	Relative level of complexity, uncertainty (often proportional with time lines), and interrelationships between processes	20%

Evaluation Criteria	Description of Evaluation Criteria	Weight
Value Discipline Fit	Relative fit to value disciplines	15%
Technology Fit	Relative tools and people capabilities to address the problem	15%
Data Fit	Relative availability of data	10%
Applicability Fit	Relative demand and usage of the solution	5%

In the sample evaluation criteria shown in Exhibit 5.6, the mining company placed a high value on the potential ROI for the analytic solution and less value on data availability because it had the ability to either generate or obtain new data. Other organizations may weigh the criteria very differently.

Example: Evaluation Rubric

The next task is to develop a rubric for the evaluation criteria. This will provide consistency in scoring the potential analytic solutions. Exhibit 5.7 illustrates how qualitative criterion can be specified. Quantitative criterion is often scored based on ranges. Note that the mining company chose to use qualitative criteria for the business value at this point because it didn't want to slow down the process by performing a formal business plan that would have provided hard data for ROI.

Exhibit 5.7   Scoring Rubric

Score	Business Value Fit	Industry Need Fit	Value Discipline Fit	Technology Fit	Data Fit	Applicability Fit
1	No return or no cost, throughput, or recovery driver	Well-known problem with well-defined solutions	Satisfies only tertiary driver	No knowledge	Mostly unknown data sources	
2	Important cost, throughput, or recovery driver			Domain knowledge or technical approach understood	Some unknown data sources	Strategic
3		High-level complexity and many variables	Satisfies secondary driver	Software artifacts available	Mostly known data sources	Managerial
4	High throughput or recovery driver	High level of uncertainty in decision making	Satisfies only primary driver	Library artifacts Available	Known and/or identifiable data sources	
5	High risk/return (throughput, recovery, or cost) driver	High-level trade-offs of process inter-relationships	Satisfies primary and secondary drivers	Software available and no further development necessary	Known and available data sources	Operational

Step 6: Evaluate Analytic Solution Opportunities

After you establish the rubric, work with stakeholders to score the potential analytic opportunities. This can be done collectively or through a process by which individuals score and the results are combined.

Example: Scored Decision Model

At that point, the weighting criteria are applied to determine weighted scores for each potential solution. The list of potential solutions can be sorted in rank order of the weighted score (see Exhibit 5.8).

Now that there is consensus among stakeholders, the next step is to factor in budget and timeline. You could do this using a few approaches:

- **Top-down approach**—In this approach, management establishes a budget and timeline; for example, a three-year budget of $10 million.

- **Bottom-up planning**—In this approach, each potential solution is scoped and estimated to establish a timeline and total budget.

- **Combination top-down and bottom-up**—In this approach, a maximum budget and elapsed time are established, and the potential solutions are "fit" into budget and timeline.

Exhibit 5.8   Scored Decision Model

Opportunity	Business Value Fit	Industry Need Fit	Value Discipline Fit	Technology Fit	Data Fit	Applicability Fit	Total Weighted Score
Mill Optimization	5	5	5	2	5	5	4.55
Asset Maintenance Optimization	4	5	5	4	5	5	4.5
Stockpile Management Optimization	5	3	3	4	4	5	4.05
Short-Term Mine Planning Optimization	4	4	5	2	5	5	4
Asset Investment Optimization	4	3	4	4	4	5	3.85
Capital Asset Portfolio Optimization	4	5	5	2	3	2	3.85
Mobile Equipment Fleet Optimization	4	3	5	2	5	5	3.8
Exploration & Early Development Portfolio Optimization	5	4	4	1	4	2	3.8
Inbound Logistics Optimization	3	5	4	4	4	2	3.75
Crush & Screen Modeling	4	3	4	2	5	5	3.65

Opportunity	Business Value Fit	Industry Need Fit	Value Discipline Fit	Technology Fit	Data Fit	Applicability Fit	Total Weighted Score
Sales Opportunity Optimization	3	4	4	4	4	3	3.6
Crew Roster Optimization	3	5	2	4	5	3	3.6
Integrated Planning Optimization	2	5	5	5	2	2	3.5
Geostatistical Modeling	4	3	3	2	5	5	3.5
Market Simulation	5	2	3	4	2	2	3.5
Beneficiation Process Optimization	3	4	5	1	5	5	3.5
Life of Mine Optimization	3	5	5	1	4	2	3.45
Scenario Planning Optimization	3	5	4	2	4	2	3.45

Example: Day-in-Life-of-Scenario

You can define a potential project in many ways, each of which takes a varying amount of time and effort to complete. A relatively quick way to define a project is to create Day-in-the-Life-of-Scenarios that describe the most typical events that occur for each potential solution. This provides enough specificity to scope the project for project estimation purposes (see Exhibits 5.9a through 5.9c).

The following is a checklist of questions to be addressed in each scenario:

- What is the context—situation, complications, and resolution—of the scenario in the overall business?
- What is the goal of the scenario?
- What are the business issues?
- What are the pre-existing conditions, constraints, and dependencies, if any?
- What are the triggers for the scenario?
- What are the bottlenecks, if any?
- What are any applicable business rules?
- What are the alternative scenarios that could be triggered, if any?
- What are the significant business consequences?
- What are the integration points, if any?
- Who are the key stakeholders in the scenario?
- What business areas or stakeholders, internally and externally, are affected by the scenario?
- What are the economic and/or operational benefits?

Rail Optimization

1.1 Scenario: Throughput Maximization

1.1.1 Situation

Rail operations are a bottleneck and with strong commodity prices, every bit of additional throughput from greater asset utilization becomes incremental revenue that goes straight to the bottom line.

1.1.2 Complication

Rail operations are highly dependent upon a high number of associated activities and are an integral part of the production and blending processes. Rail is highly capital intensive and has long lead-times on new assets. Customers need solutions that can optimize the current asset base.

1.1.3 Resolution

The solution is an integrated planning tool to assist planners in making complex, multi-objective trade-off decisions to deliver an optimal rail plan and thereby adding value to the business. This rail plan will optimize both ore throughput as well as asset utilization.

1.1.4 Scenario Description: Throughput Maximization

Rail operations are often a bottleneck for the integrated operations of a rapidly growing, demand-driven mining company, where a key to success is optimizing production output. Additional capacity for the rail operations can be added through the purchase of additional consists.[2] The overarching constraints on the rail operations include

---

[2] A consist is a sequence of locomotives and ore cars, and is defined differently for each customer.

- The loading and unloading at the mine (point of origin) and the port (destination)
- The physical infrastructure currently in operation (that is, single track, passing lanes, and so on)
- Staffing availability
- Port or mine blending requirements
- Maintenance requirements—planned vs. unplanned

Exhibit 5.9a Day-in-the-Life-of-Scenario

The goal of the rail operations is to fully utilize the maximum capacity of the rail infrastructure while satisfying the production plan, which includes tonnage, quality, and safety considerations.

Key bottlenecks in the process include

- Availability of product at loading point
- Availability of trucks at loading and dumping at the port
- Availability of passing tracks
- Preventative and break-fix maintenance of the rail assets
- Availability of drivers/operators
- Capacity constraints of source & destination stockpiles
- Scheduling of product mix before transportation

The multi-objective rail throughput optimizer:

- Minimizes idle time waiting for passing trains
- Minimizes turnaround time
- Minimizes dumping and loading time
- Minimizes maintenance downtime
- Minimizes the number of trucks required
- Maximizes the load within each dumper
- Maximizes the load for the consist

Inefficient rail operations result in significant financial losses (each lost consist equates to a several million dollars loss).

The rail optimization integrates with several key systems including

- Asset maintenance
- Operations planning
- Mining production for origin stockpiles
- Port operations for destination stockpiles

The key stakeholders include Operations, Mining Production, Port Operations, Asset Maintenance, Marketing, and Sales.

An optimized rail operations results in

- Increased revenue
- Decreased capital spending or deferring capital expenditures
- Reduced maintenance cost
- Reduced operating cost
- Increased safety
- Reduced carbon emission
- Reduced total material moved (TTM)

In summary, the key business questions to be answered by the solution for this scenario are

- When do we really need to be spending money on capital investments?
- What types of locomotives and ore cars should we purchase to maximize throughput and minimize cost?
- What should be our consist make-up (2 vs. 3 locomotives and where in the consist)?
- How effective are our maintenance strategies?
- What is the right balance/roster of resources to maximize throughput and production targets?

Exhibit 5.9b   Day-in-the-Life-of-Scenario

- Where do I need to focus on my efforts/bottleneck busting?
- What is the best configuration for our locomotives?
- What is the minimum stockpile capacity I need to guarantee throughput?
- How much is my blending costing me in throughput?
- Given the current equipment, how do we maximize tonnes carried by rail (frequency, tonnes moved per cycle)?
- How do we balance rail optimization across different mine sites?
- What is the ideal size of the fleet?
- What is the best design for the fleet?
- What is the best utilization of the optimized design?

1.1.5 Key Business Requirements

Constraints include

- Stockpile capacity
- Resource capacity
- Maximum allowable load for train and consist
- Number of trucks available per location (origins & destinations)
- Target product blend
- Maximum rail hours

The solution delivers the following reports:

- A time-sequenced optimized rail plan by site and by consist
- A rail operator schedule including number of operators required by shift
- A product blend schedule for each of the mines included in the scope of the optimization

- Maintenance schedule by consist and loco by job
- Track maintenance plan

1.1.6 Desired Outcomes

A 3–6 month optimized plan for the rail operations given the current strategic physical asset constraints.

Exhibit 5.9c Day-in-the-Life-of-Scenario

Step 7: Establish Analytics Roadmap

Using the budgetary and timeline constraints plus the high-level analytic solution descriptions, you can create a rough-cut estimate of budget and project time for each of the potential analytic solutions.

Example: Rough-Cut Project Estimate

Exhibit 5.10 shows a rough-cut project estimate for the mining example used throughout this chapter.

Exhibit 5.10 Rough-Cut Project Estimate

Opportunity	Total Weighted Score	Est. Budget	Est. Elapsed Time
Mill Optimization	4.55	$500,000	9
Asset Maintenance Optimization	4.5	$1,000,000	18
Stockpile Management Optimization	4.05	$250,000	3
Short-Term Mine Planning Optimization	4	$350,000	4
Asset Investment Optimization	3.85	$200,000	2
Capital Asset Portfolio Optimization	3.85	$150,000	2

Opportunity	Total Weighted Score	Est. Budget	Est. Elapsed Time
Mobile Equipment Fleet Optimization	3.8	$1,700,000	24
Exploration & Early Development Portfolio Optimization	3.8	$400,000	9

Example: Analytic Solution Roadmap

Using the example of the three-year $3 million budget, the first six projects in Exhibit 5.10 were selected because they are the highest priorities and are within the $3 million budget (total of $2.45 million). However, the next highest priority project, Mobile Equipment Fleet Optimization, was eliminated because the cost ($1.7 million) of adding it would exceed the budget cost ($1.7 million). The same is true for the next two projects, but although the Crush & Screen project slightly exceeded the budget, after discussion it was decided to include it in the roadmap as a possibility. Using this information, an analytics roadmap for the organization is set as shown in Exhibit 5.11.

This is only one way to determine the potential analytic solution projects. Another way would be to use a spiral methodology[3] to create smaller scope projects that deliver initial results with subsequent phases that build on those initial successes. By using this approach, you can start and complete more projects earlier, which allows business impact and project lessons to be realized quicker.

[3] See Barry Boehm, "Spiral Development: Experience, Principles, and Refinements," Special Report CMU/SEI-2000-SR-008 (July 2000), http://www.sei.cmu.edu/reports/00sr008.pdf.

Exhibit 5-11 Analytic Solution Roadmap

Analytic Solution	Est. Budget	Q1	Q2	Q3	Q4	Q1	Q2
Mill Optimization	$500,000	9 months					
Asset Maintenance Optimization	$1,000,000	18 months					
Stockpile Management Optimization	$250,000			3 months			
Short-Term Mine Planning Optimization	$350,000				4 months		
Asset Investment Optimization	$200,000		2 months				
Capital Asset Portfolio Optimization	$150,000					2 months	
Exploration & Early Development Portfolio Optimization	$400,000				9 months		
Crush & Screen Modeling	$175,000						2 months
Total Budget	$3,025,000						

Step 8: Evolve Your Analytics Roadmap

Your unique analytics roadmap is an evolving blueprint for what you're planning to implement to use analytics as a strategic lever to drive business value and impact in your business. To persist the roadmap, you'll need to update and revise your roadmap periodically. The frequency of updates depends on how quickly your business executes on the roadmap. If you're a fast-growing organization with superb execution skills, you'll pulse faster and will need to update your roadmap more frequently. You'll want to update your roadmap as your business needs are constantly changing in reaction to the marketplace and that may impact your roadmap. Technology is changing rapidly, and those changes may impact the feasibility of some of the efforts on your roadmap. Build a closed-loop change process into your roadmap and be sure to share the updates with your extended team so everyone stays aligned with the current state of the roadmap.

Each project on your analytics roadmap has stated goals. As part of the project readiness for deployment, the actual performance and business impact will be measured and compared to the stated goals until the goals are achieved or surpassed. After the production deployment, you should establish new goals and objectives that drive toward continual improvements. For any analytic project that failed, you should perform a thorough analysis of why the project failed so that you can learn and avoid the same mistakes in future projects.

Summary

To build your unique analytics roadmap, follow these steps:

Step 1   Identify key business objectives.

Step 2   Define your value chain.

Step 3   Brainstorm analytic solution opportunities.

Step 4   Describe analytic solution opportunities.

Step 5   Create decision model.

Step 6   Evaluate analytic solution opportunities.

Step 7   Establish analytics roadmap.

Step 8   Evolve your analytics roadmap
         Day-in-the-Life-of-Scenario

6

Analytic Applications

Overview

Analytics is a broad topic (see Exhibit 6.1); there are many ways to categorize enterprise analytics. In this chapter, we describe different types of *primary demand* for analytics; furthermore, we examine how this affects organization choices of analytic methods and tooling. A key premise of this chapter is that there is no *single* set of methods and tooling that meets every need; consequently, the key question that must drive analytic decision making at all levels is: *What are we going to do with the results?*

We categorize enterprise analytics into five groups:

- **Strategic Analytics**—Analytics for top management
- **Managerial Analytics**—Analytics for functional leadership
- **Operational Analytics**—Analytics that support a business process
- **Scientific Analytics**—Analytics that support the development of new knowledge
- **Customer-Facing Analytics**—Analytics for the end consumer

In the chapters that follow, we describe each of these categories in more detail, with working examples.

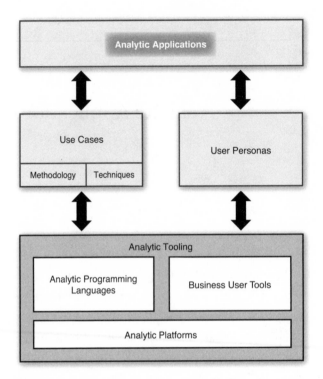

Exhibit 6.1   Modern Analytics Framework

Strategic Analytics

Strategic analytics addresses the decision support needs of an organization's top management: the "C-suite." Strategic analytics addresses strategic issues and questions.

What makes an issue strategic? Strategic questions and issues have four distinct characteristics. First, the *stakes are high*; there are major consequences that depend on the right answers. Second, strategic issues fall *outside existing policy*; there is no established rule that enables decisions at a lower level. Third, strategic issues tend to be *nonrepeatable*; in most cases, the organization addresses a strategic question once and never again. Fourth, there is *no clear consensus* among leadership about the best way forward; uncertainty prevails, and management factions disagree about key facts. (If there is no disagreement, there is no need for analysis.)

Examples of strategic questions include

- Should we continue to invest in an underperforming line of business?
- How will a proposed acquisition affect our business?
- What economic climate do we expect next year? How will this affect our sales?
- Why is our top-selling SUV involved in so many rollover accidents?

Because executives rely on strategic analytics to establish consensus, the value of the analysis depends more on the credibility and record of accomplishment of the analyst (rather than on methodological precision or theoretical elegance). The independence of the analyst is also key, especially so if the analysis will be used to resolve differences among management factions. Speed is often essential; the world will not wait for analysis.

Although the issue at hand may be a "one-off" for the firm, other firms may have faced similar circumstances; experience with similar situations elevates the value of outside consultants compared to internal analysts. Moreover, answers to strategic questions frequently require data that is not readily accessible and may be outside the organization.

For all these reasons—independence, credibility, record of accomplishment, urgency, and external data—enterprises tend to depend heavily on outside consultants for strategic analytics. However, analytic leaders establish an internal team for strategic analytics that operates outside of traditional functional silos. In the sections that follow, we describe some common applications and techniques.

Ad Hoc Analysis

Organizations invest a surprisingly large amount of time and effort doing ad hoc analysis. *Ad hoc analysis* is a term that applies to the practice of acquiring new data pertinent to a particular question and performing relatively simple analysis: joining tables, summarizing data, computing simple statistics, preparing graphs, and so forth.

Software industry analysts often find this practice perplexing because ad hoc analysis does not follow standard business intelligence practice. Business intelligence systems based on modern data warehousing work very well for lower-level decisions that are repeatable, historically based, and operable within a policy framework. Conventional business intelligence does not work well or at all for the non-repeatable questions and issues escalated to the C-suite. Ad hoc analysis fills the gap between the needs of top management and the capabilities of the business intelligence system.

Successful ad hoc analysis requires a different breed of analysts. This type of work tends to attract highly experienced and capable analysts who are able to work rapidly and accurately under pressure. Backgrounds tend to be eclectic: A leading insurance company, for example, has a strategic analysis team that includes an anthropologist, an economist, an epidemiologist, and a highly experienced claims specialist.

Successful strategic ad hoc analysts develop domain, business, and organizational expertise that lend credibility to their work. Above all, successful analysts take a skeptical approach to the data and demonstrate the necessary drive and initiative to get answers. This often means doing hard things, such as working with programming tools and granular data to find the underlying cause of a problem.

Successful teams operate outside of the IT organization. Conventional IT production standards are neither necessary nor appropriate for ad hoc analytics, where flexibility and agility are key to success.

Successful organizations recognize this and allow analysts some latitude in how they organize and manage data.

Analytic tooling for strategic analysis tends to reflect the diverse backgrounds of the analytics and varies widely. Strategic analysts use Structured Query Language (SQL), SAS, or R to do the work and use standard office productivity tools to deliver results. (One of the most effective strategy analysts we know uses nothing other than SQL and Excel.) Because strategic analysis teams tend to be small, there is little value in demanding use of a single tool set; moreover, most analysts want to use the best tool for the job and prefer to use niche tools optimized for a single problem.

The most important common requirement for a strategic analytics team is the capability to rapidly ingest and organize data from any source and in any format. For many organizations, this has historically meant using SAS. (A surprisingly large number of analytic teams use SAS to ingest and organize the data, but perform the actual analysis using other tools.) Growing data volumes, however, pose a performance challenge for the conventional SAS architecture, so analytic teams increasingly look to data warehouse appliances from vendors such as IBM, Teradata, Pivotal, or Hadoop.

Strategic Market Segmentation

Market segmentation is both a strategy pursued at the highest levels of the organization and a set of analytic techniques used to support formulation of the strategy. The two are sometimes confused. Organizations can apply the analytic techniques to tactical targeted marketing; in that case, the internal clients are junior managers. The clients for strategic market segmentation analysis are the chief marketing officer (CMO) and other members of the C-suite.

Businesses segment the market when they develop new products, enter new markets, or reinvigorate a product line that has saturated its markets. By dividing a broader market into distinct groups with distinct needs or communication habits, businesses define ways to solve customer problems more effectively and build loyalty.

In most cases, the goal of strategic market segmentation is to define better ways to reach consumers who are not customers; segmentation analysis usually includes external data captured from surveys or secondary sources. Outside consultants tend to perform the work because they have the specialized expertise needed to deliver a credible segmentation analysis and because the work is generally too infrequent to justify an in-house capability.

Econometric Forecasting

In many organizations, periodic planning and budgeting begins with an assessment of the economic climate expected over the planning horizon. Rather than simply guessing about the future, executives rely heavily on econometric forecasting for baseline predictions about such things as economic growth, inflation, currency movements, and so forth.

Econometricians use advanced mathematics, statistics, and high-powered computers to construct complex models of the economy and then use these models to develop forecasts for key measures. Because it is very expensive to build and maintain these models, only the largest organizations build their own econometric models. Instead, most organizations subscribe to forecasts produced by firms such as IHS Global Insight and then use analysis to link their own key measures to the purchased economic indicators.

Business Simulation

Econometric models use advanced mathematics to model complex large-scale systems. These methods work reasonably well when the goal is to forecast measures that align well with key economic indicators. For example, a national department store chain may find that its own retail sales correlate well with forecasts of aggregate household consumption spending.

Although the point estimates produced by an econometric forecast are useful for strategic planning, in many cases the executive suite is more concerned with the range of possible outcomes and not simply a forecast. Executives may be concerned about the behavior of certain well-defined processes (such as a manufacturing operation) or set of assets (such as a book of insurance policies or an investment portfolio). In these circumstances, business simulation is a useful application.

Business simulation is the mathematical representation of a real-world system over time. Simulation depends on initial construction of a mathematical model that represents the key characteristics or behaviors of the selected system or process. The model represents the system, whereas a simulation represents operation of the system over time with a given set of assumptions.

Because managers can vary the assumptions, business simulation is an excellent tool for "what-if" analysis. For example, a life insurance company can simulate its financial results under different sets of assumptions about policyholder behavior, mortality, and conditions in the financial markets. Managers can use the results of simulation to make decisions about whether or not to get into a certain line of business, acquire another carrier, reinsure the portfolio, or make other decisions with strategic consequences.

Northern Trust, a global financial institution headquartered in Chicago, Illinois, uses Monte Carlo simulation to assess operational risk. Governed by federal law and international standards, risk assessment is a highly visible task; top-level executives rely on the analysis to set policies for asset quality and portfolio strategy. Risk analysts use Revolution R Enterprise, a commercial distribution of open source R, to simulate financial outcomes under a wide range of economic scenarios. For any single scenario, analysts run simulations consisting of millions of iterations.

Managerial Analytics

Analytic applications serving the needs of middle managers focus on specific functions:

- What is the best way to manage our cash?
- Is product XYZ performing according to expectations?
- How effective are our marketing programs?
- Where can we find the best opportunities for new retail outlets?

There are differences in nomenclature across functions, as well as distinct opportunities for specialized analytics (such as store location analysis, marketing mix analysis, new product forecasting, and so on). Managerial questions and issues tend to fall into three categories:

- Measuring the results of existing entities (products, programs, stores, factories, and so on)
- Optimizing the performance of existing entities
- Planning and developing new entities

Measuring existing entities with reports, dashboards, drill-everywhere, and so on is the sweet spot for enterprise business intelligence (BI) systems. Such systems are highly effective when the data is timely and credible, reports are easy to use, and the system reflects a meaningful assessment framework. This means that metrics (activity, revenue, costs, and profits) reflect the goals of the business function and enable comparison across entities.

Given the state of BI technology, analysis teams within functions (marketing, underwriting, store operations, and so on) spend a surprisingly large amount of time preparing routine reports for managers. (For example, an insurance client asked for an assessment of actual work performed by a group of more than 100 SAS users. The client was astonished to learn that it could easily reproduce most of the SAS reports in Cognos, which it also owned.)

In some cases, reports consume analyst time because the organization lacks investment in the necessary tools and enablers, a problem that is easily fixed. More often than not, though, the root cause is the absence of consensus about measurement standards. In organizations that lack measurement discipline, assessment is a chaotic situation in which individual program and product managers seek out customized reports that show their program or product to the best advantage. In this environment, every program or product is a winner, and analytics loses credibility with management. There is no technical "fix" for this problem; it takes leadership from management to set out clear goals for the organization and build consensus for an assessment framework.

Functional analysts often complain that they spend so much time preparing routine reports that they have little or no time to perform analytics that optimize the performance of existing entities. (Optimization technology is not new, but organizations are slow to adopt it for managerial analytics.) Functionally focused optimization tools for management decisions have been available for more than a decade, but adoption is limited for several reasons:

- First, an organization stuck in the "ad hoc" trap described in the previous paragraph will never build the kind of history needed to optimize anything.

- Second, managers at this level tend to be overly optimistic about the value of their own judgment in business decisions and resist efforts to replace intuitive judgment with systematic and metrics-based optimization.

- Finally, in areas such as marketing mix decisions, constrained optimization necessarily means choosing one entity over another for resources; this is inherently a leadership decision.

Analytics for planning and developing new entities (such as programs, products, or stores) usually requires information from outside the organization and may require skills not present in existing staff.

For both reasons, organizations often outsource this function to providers with access to pertinent skills and data. For analysts inside the organization, technical requirements look a lot like those for strategic analytics: the ability to ingest data quickly from any source combined with a flexible and agile programming environment and functional support for a wide range of generic analytic problems.

Marketing attribution analysis is an excellent example of managerial analytics. Attribution analysis uses historical data and advanced analytics to link customer buying behavior with marketing programs and impressions. In a simpler world before the explosion of e-commerce and digital marketing, marketers relied on aggregate analysis of media markets to assess advertising impact. With the marketing mix shifting to digital media, marketing executives rely on attribution modeling at the individual consumer level to measure the effectiveness of individual programs and communications. Attribution analysis enables organizations to save money, increase revenue per campaign, and customize each customer's relationship with the company.

Operational Analytics

This section covers operational analytics, defined as analytics that improve the efficiency or effectiveness of a business process. The distinction between managerial and operational analytics can be subtle, and generally boils down to the level of aggregation and frequency of the analysis. For example, the CMO is interested in understanding the performance and ROI of all marketing programs but is unlikely to be interested in the operational details of any one program. The manager of that program, however, may be intensely interested in its operational details but have no interest in the performance of other programs.

Differences in level of aggregation and frequency lead to qualitative differences in the types of analytics that are pertinent. A CMO's interest in programs is typically at a level of "keep or kill": Continue funding the program if it is effective, kill it if it is not. This kind of problem is well suited to dashboard-style BI combined with solid revenue attribution and ROI metrics. The program manager, on the other hand, is intensely interested in a range of metrics that shed insight not simply on how well the program is performing, but why it is performing as it is and how to improve it. Moreover, the program manager in this example will be deeply involved in operational decisions such as selecting the target audience, determining which offers to assign, handling response exceptions, and managing delivery to schedule and budget. This is the realm of operational analytics.

Although any BI package can handle different levels of aggregation and cadence, the very diverse nature of operational detail across business processes makes the problem more complex. A social media-marketing program relies on data sources and operational systems that are entirely different from web media or email marketing programs. Preapproved and non-preapproved credit card acquisition programs do not use the same systems to assign credit lines; some or all of these processes may be outsourced. Few enterprises have successfully rationalized all of their operational data into a single enterprise data store (nor is it likely they will ever do so). As a result, it is very rare that a common BI system comprehensively supports both managerial and operational analytic needs. More typically, one system supports managerial analytics (for one or more disciplines), while diverse systems and ad hoc analysis support operational analytics.

At this level, questions tend to be domain-specific and analysts are highly specialized in that domain. Hence, an analyst who is an expert in search engine optimization is not qualified to perform credit risk analysis. This has little to do with the analytic methods used, which tend to be similar across business disciplines, and more to do with the language and lingo used in the discipline as well as domain-specific technology and regulatory issues. A biostatistician must understand common healthcare data formats and HIPAA regulations; a consumer credit risk analysis must understand FICO scores, FISERV formats, and FCRA. In both cases, the analyst must have or develop a deep understanding of the organization's business processes because this is essential to recognizing opportunities for improvement and prioritizing analytic projects.

Although analytics might improve business processes in a plethora of different ways, most applications fall in to one of three categories:

1. Applied decision systems support business processes through better decisions at scale. Examples include customer-requested line increases or credit card transaction authorization systems. These applications improve the business process by applying consistent data-driven rules designed to balance risks and rewards. Analytics embedded in such systems help the organization optimize the trade-off between "loose" and "tight" criteria and ensure that decision criteria reflect actual experience. An analytics-driven decision system performs in a faster and more consistent way than systems based on human decisions, and considers more information than a human decision-maker considers.

2. Targeting and routing systems speed transaction handling by automating referrals. An example of this is a text-processing system that reads each incoming email and routes it to the appropriate customer service specialist. Whereas applied decision systems in the first category tend to recommend categorical yes/no, approve/decline decisions in a stream of transactions, a targeting system selects from a larger pool of candidates and may make qualitative decisions among a large number of alternate routings. The business benefit from this kind of system is improved productivity and reduced processing time as, for example, the organization no longer requires a team to read every email and route it to the appropriate specialist. Applied analytics makes these systems possible.

3. Operational forecasting systems project key metrics that affect operations. An example of this is a system that uses projected store traffic to determine staffing levels. These systems enable the organization to operate more efficiently through better alignment of operations to customer demand. Again, applied analytics makes such systems possible; while it is theoretically possible to build such a system without an analytic forecasting component, it is inconceivable that any management would place operations at the mercy of guesswork. Unlike the first two applications, forecasting systems often work with aggregate data rather than atomic data.

For analytic reporting, the ability to ingest data rapidly from operational data sources (internal and external) is critical, as is the ability to publish reports into a broad-based reporting and BI presentation system.

Deployability is the key requirement for predictive analytics; the analyst must be able to publish a predictive model as a Predictive Model Markup Language (PMML) document or as executable code in a choice of programming languages.

Scientific Analytics

The previous sections on strategic, managerial, and operational analytics covered categories of analytics in which managers at various levels rely on analytics to make decisions. Scientific analytics, the subject of this section, supports a completely different purpose: the production of new knowledge.

There are two distinctly different kinds of scientific knowledge. Public knowledge is freely available, funded by universities and governments. Private knowledge is different; intellectual property laws protect property rights, and private capital invests in knowledge intent on developing a commercial product. Due to the high potential returns on successful intellectual property, the investment in analytics for private knowledge (such as biotechnology, pharmaceuticals, and clinical research) accounts for a large share of total spending on analytics.

Scientific analysts are highly concerned about using analytic methods that can withstand scrutiny from peer review; this concern tends to drive their choice of techniques. They also tend to be much more concerned about understanding causes of variance than with prediction; this contrasts sharply with other commercial applications, where accurate prediction tends to be of primary concern.

The State University of New York (SUNY) at Buffalo is home to one of the leading multiple sclerosis (MS) research centers in the world. The SUNY team works with genomic data from MS patients to identify genes whose variations could contribute to the risk of developing MS. Because gene products work by interacting with both other gene products and environmental factors, the team is interested in researching combinations of interacting genes.

The data sets used in genomic research are very large, and the analysis is computationally complex because the researchers are looking for interactions between thousands of genetic and environmental factors; due to combinatorial explosion, there could be quintillions of possible effects to measure. The SUNY Buffalo team uses Revolution R Enterprise together with an IBM PureData System for Analytics appliance to simplify and speed up very complex analysis on very big data sets.

Customer-Facing Analytics

For lack of a better term, we refer to the last category of analytics as *customer-facing analytics,* which we define as analytics that differentiate products by solving problems for end consumers.

As noted previously, managers at various levels frequently use outside providers to satisfy analytic needs for various reasons. Often, however, the methods and techniques employed by the outside provider are the same as what an internal team could provide. When the outside consultant simply serves as staff augmentation, we do not consider that a fundamentally different form of analytics.

Customer-facing analytics differentiates products from alternatives to create unique value in the marketplace. There are three distinct categories of customer-facing analytics:

- Prediction services
- Analytic applications
- Consumer analytics

Next, we discuss each of these categories.

Prediction Services

For conventional analytic consulting services, the "product" sold and delivered is an analysis project; pricing depends on the consulting hours required to complete the project and the time-value of resources consumed. For prediction services, the product sold and delivered to the customer is a prediction, not a project; pricing depends on the number of predictions used. Credit scores are the best-known example of prediction services, but there are many other examples of prediction services for sales, marketing, human resources, and insurance underwriting.

Organizations can satisfy demand for prediction services with internally developed models or purchased models; from a technical perspective, the predictive model may be the same. However, externally developed prediction services tend to work in a very different way. External developers amortize costs of predictive models over many transactions, so prediction services enable a broad market of smaller enterprises to benefit from predictive analytics that would not be able to do so otherwise. Prediction service providers are also able to achieve economies of scale and often have access to data sources that would not necessarily be available to the enterprise.

Analytic Applications

Analytic applications are a natural extension of prediction services. Analytic applications are business applications that consume data-driven predictions and support all or part of a business process. Examples include

- Mortgage application decision systems (which consume predictions about the applicant's propensity to repay the loan)
- Insurance underwriting systems (which consume predictions about expected losses from an insurance policy)
- Fraud case management systems (which consume predictions about the likelihood that a particular claim or group of claims is fraudulent)

Developers often sell and deliver these applications under a "razor-and-blade" strategy, where the application itself carries a fixed price combined with a long-term contract to provide prediction services.

The [x+1] platform is branded as the Origin Programmatic Marketing Hub and is designed to make digital marketing more effective for brands and more relevant to consumers. The platform includes exchange-based display ad buying combined with tools for data management, site decision making, tag management, and mobile advertising.

The core of [x+1]'s platform is a centralized decision engine called the Predictive Optimization Engine (POE™), which utilizes

Revolution R Enterprise, and leverages both proprietary and third-party data managed by its Big Data Framework. POE™ targets the best audiences across channels and individually tailors messages by site and visitor in real-time.

Consumer Analytics

Each of the first two categories of analytic products is similar to and competes with "in-house" delivered strategic, managerial, and operational analytics. The third category, consumer analytics, is potentially the most disruptive and offers enterprises the greatest potential return. Consumer analytics differentiates the firm's products in meaningful ways by solving a consumer problem:

- Consumers have a problem finding information. Google's search engine—text mining applied on a massive scale—solves this problem.
- Consumers have a problem finding a movie they want to watch. Netflix's recommendation engine solves this problem.

These examples—and many others, including Facebook's news-feed engine and Match.com's matching algorithm—use machine learning technology in ways that directly benefit customers. However, the firms that offer these services benefit indirectly, by building site traffic, selling more product, or satisfying customers in a manner that competitors cannot easily reproduce.

Summary

In this chapter, we described different types of analytics according to the organizational role of the analytics consumer. We discussed how the analytics consumer's role affects key characteristics of the analytics project, including timeliness and repeatability, and how these characteristics influence the choice of tools and methods.

As noted at the beginning of the chapter, the analyst must ask at the beginning of each project: *Who will use this analysis? What are we going to do with the results?*

7

Analytic Use Cases

Overview

In the preceding chapter, we summarized key applications for analytics according to the organizational role of those who consume the analytic insights. In this chapter, we view analytics from a different perspective: We categorize analytics according to generic use cases that share common objectives, actors, methods, and technology (see Exhibit 7.1). In doing so, we discuss the implications of scaling and cadence—the need to address larger problems and to do so more rapidly.

In systems and software engineering, a *use case* is a description of steps required to meet an objective. Understanding analytic use cases is a critical success factor for organizations seeking to define analytics architecture.

There is a many-to-many relationship between analytic use cases and analytic applications. Business applications, such as targeted marketing and credit risk, are examples of the prediction use case; however, a targeted marketing application may incorporate other use cases, such as segmentation and graph analysis.

The use case model is a convenient way to describe processes shared by analysts across the organization, even though they may support very different business applications.

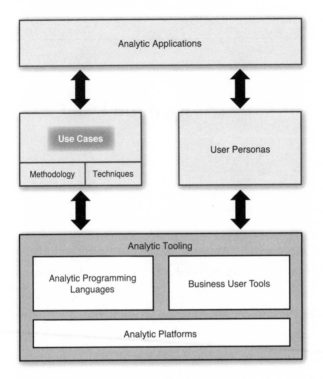

Exhibit 7.1 Modern Analytics Framework

Exhibit 7.2 shows analytic applications organized by use cases and the application classes we discussed in the previous chapter.

We distinguish use cases from one another if the methodologies are materially different. While the Prediction and Explanation use cases described next share many techniques, they have fundamentally different goals and output.

It is important to understand your organization's analytic use cases because the efficiency and effectiveness of your analytic architecture depends on how well you understand the underlying processes. Applications that share use cases can share technology, offering opportunities to save money. On the other hand, distinct use cases may require unique tools and techniques.

Exhibit 7.2   Applications and Use Cases

Use Cases	Applications				
	Strategic	Managerial	Operational	Scientific	Customer-Facing
Prediction	Catastrophic Risk Analysis	Marketing Campaign Planning	Credit Scoring	Side Effects Prediction	Sports Odds
Explanation	Marketing Mix Analysis	Marketing Attribution Analysis	Defect Analysis	Genetic Trait Analysis	Credit Decline Explanation
Forecasting	Strategic Planning	Annual Budgeting	Store Staffing Optimization	Climate Forecasting	
Discovery					
Text and Document Processing		Content Management	Inbound Email Routing	Plagiarism Detection	Document Search
Segmentation	Strategic Market Segmentation	Tactical Market Segmentation		Psychographic Research	
Association		Market Basket Analysis	Matching		Recommenders
Outlier Detection			Network Threat Detection		
Graph/Network Analysis		Social Network Analysis	Fraud Detection	Criminology	Social Matching
Simulation	Business Scenario Analysis	Value At Risk Analysis	Marketing Campaign Simulation	Climate Modeling	
Optimization	Capital Asset Optimization	Marketing Mix Optimization	Campaign Offer Optimization	Particle Swarm Optimization	Agricultural Yield Optimization

In the following sections, we describe the most common analytic use cases at the highest level. In Chapter 8, "Predictive Analytics Methodology," we describe methodology for the predictive analytics use case in detail.

Prediction

Within the Prediction use case, we distinguish between the Model Building and the Model Scoring subcases. Both parts are essential and directed toward the same goal, but Model Scoring often engages different actors in the organization and usually has different technology requirements.

Building predictive models is the classic use case for analytics; it is the foundation of a wide range of established applications for marketing, credit risk management, and a wide range of other business disciplines. In later chapters, we cover methods and techniques for predictive analytics in detail.

Most people intuitively understand that more data necessarily means better analysis. In many cases, however, analysts can build a perfectly good model by sampling from a larger database. There are three specific ways that an expanded analytic data set creates new problems and opportunities for the analyst:

- **More cases, observations, or rows**—This creates opportunities for analysts to segment the population and build specialized models for each segment, leading to better overall predictions. Where sampling is used, larger samples reduce the sampling error of the model and increase model precision.

- **More variables, features, or columns**—By searching across more potential predictors, analysts can improve predictive models by identifying variables with incremental information value.

- **Many small models**—In this scenario, the problem consists of bulk analysis for many small *a priori* segments (for example, stores, holdings, or customers).

The three types of problems have different implications for the tools analysts require. Organizations manage the added workload from case expansion by eliminating data movement, using parallel processing, and employing other techniques that improve overall performance. *Ensemble modeling* techniques simplify the task of building segmented models for subgroups within the overall population.

To address columnar expansion, on the other hand, analysts must use *dimension reduction* techniques (such as feature selection or feature extraction) and techniques designed to handle high-dimension data. *Regularization* and *stepwise* methods are useful enhancements to regression when working with wide data sets. Analytic software should be able to support large sparse matrices for good performance with a wide data set.

Analysts increasingly seek to build large quantities of models, numbering in the thousands and more. Each model may use relatively small amounts of data, but taken as a whole, the data set required for all models is very large. The following are some examples:

- An analytic services provider builds more than a thousand consumer "propensity to buy" at the SKU level for its retail clients.

- A retailer with 3,000 stores seeks to produce individual time series forecasts for every customer.

- A credit card issuer with millions of account models uses individual information about the account to model delinquency and default propensities.

- An investment bank holding millions of positions seeks to use historical data about the performance of each security to build individual behavior models.

At the level of individual models, the techniques used for the "many small models" are largely the same as those used for "one big model"; moreover, the total amount of data used may be the same. The computational workload and implications for features, however, are very different. When the number of individual models is very large, it is not possible for an analyst to build each model separately; instead, the analyst requires a *model automation wrapper* that enables the analyst to run and monitor many model-building sessions in parallel while providing reasonable confidence in the validity of the individual models.

Scoring uses a previously built model to compute predicted values for each case in the data set, either individually or in batch. Scoring is the deployment of the model and is usually embarrassingly parallel; this means that a master process can distribute tasks to worker processes for parallel execution, and the final product is a simple combination of the output from the distributed processes. Scoring is relatively easy to implement in a massively parallel processing (MPP) database when there is a way to transfer the predictive model from the analytics development environment to the production data warehouse.

We need to note a few detailed points about scoring and prediction. First, there is no necessary relationship between the size of the data set used to build a predictive model and the size of the data set for scoring—it is perfectly reasonable to build a model on a large data set and then score individual transactions in real-time as they occur. The reverse is also true: An analyst can build a model on a sample and then score a large population.

Second, analysts can build a predictive model from one database and use it for prediction with data from a different database. A credit risk analyst, for example, may use data from an enterprise data warehouse to build a delinquency model for use within an adaptive control system for credit line management. For this to work, however, the two databases must have aligned schemas; the analysis database can be a subset of the production database but cannot be a superset.

Third, prediction is not the same as decision making. Scoring is a simple computation performed with an analytic model on new data; prediction usually requires some kind of transformation of the raw score into a useful form, and automated decisions require the combination of a prediction with business rules. For example:

- A logistic regression model of delinquency applied to the data about an individual customer produces a probability between zero and one that the customer will go delinquent.
- Using historical data, the analyst determines the losses in different raw score bands.
- As a result, the analyst recommends a rule to implement in a decision system that customers with a raw score below 0.3 can receive credit line increases.

PMML, or Predictive Model Markup Language, offers a standards-based interface between predictive modeling tools and scoring applications, although many organizations continue to rely on manual recoding (into C, Java, Python, or some other language) to accomplish this model transfer. Manual conversion becomes much less attractive with increasing model volume and requirements for rapid deployment. Many databases and decision engines support the ability to import PMML documents, and Zementis offers tools and services to facilitate integration.

Just as building many models differs from building one big model, scoring many models also creates new requirements. Organizations with just a few models in production can treat the development of scoring procedures as ad hoc development projects. As the number of models increases, there is a growing need for *model management* capabilities that can track, monitor, and manage deployed models across the organization.

Explanation

We use the term *explanation* broadly as the systematic attribution of variation in one measure to other measures. In some cases, the business is primarily concerned with prediction—estimating the value of a response measure that you do not know in advance. In other cases, the business seeks to understand influences on the response measure, but prediction is not a high priority. In still other cases, the business needs both.

It is important to understand this distinction because some analytic methods support both objectives, whereas others are ideally suited to one or the other. Most statistical methods are useful for both prediction and explanation, while machine-learning methods are primarily useful for prediction only. There are also some statistical methods, such as mixed linear models, that are primarily useful for explanation but add relatively little value over simpler methods for prediction.

In response-attribution analysis, for example, the marketer's primary concern is to attribute responses or sales to marketing treatments (such as promotions or campaigns). Prediction is a byproduct of this analysis; many marketing treatments are not repeatable, so forecasting future responses is less important than gaining maximum insight about what worked and what did not work in the past.

Credit risk analysis is an example of an application in which the business may require both prediction and explanation. When deciding whether to grant credit to a customer, the lender wants the best possible predictions; however, the lender must also be able to offer customers plausible explanations when declining an application. Even when there is no formal requirement to explain a model, many managers are unwilling to trust "black box" predictions that lack a clear causal explanation.

Forecasting

Time series analysis and forecasting comprise a distinct class of analytics widely used in business and often embedded in enterprise systems for manufacturing, logistics, store operations, and so forth. Examples include

- A retailer uses time series analytics to forecast store traffic in hourly brands and uses the forecasts to schedule personnel.

- A brewer uses embedded time series analytics to predict stocking and inventory levels for more than 700 items, using the forecasts to adjust production and delivery schedules.

- An investment bank uses time series analytics to forecast prices for millions of individual holdings in its portfolio.

Most operational time series forecasting systems are in the "many small models" category and do not necessarily require working with large sets of data for individual forecasts; moreover, they tend to use relatively simple and standardized modeling techniques but require tooling to automate the learning and prediction process.

However, analysts may need to work with atomic source data that is not already in time series form. When this is the case, the analysts must perform a data preparation step to accumulate time-stamped transactions to a time series, perform date-and-time calculations, and create lagged variables for autoregressive analysis. This step may be difficult or impossible to perform in SQL, and analysts often perform this task outside the database in specialized software with a *time series utility*.

When working with a large number of time series, analysts cannot fit models individually but must rely on a *model automation wrapper* suited to time series analytics.

Time series analytics generally does not require independent scoring—analysts can simply visualize the predictions or transfer them to a consuming application. As is the case with conventional models, however, when the number of time series is large, a *model management* capability is required.

Discovery

Sometimes the analyst seeks to discover useful patterns in data, but does not require a formal prediction, explanation, or forecast. Such patterns assume a number of forms:

- Meaningful content in text or documents
- Homogeneous groups of cases
- Associations between objects
- Unusual cases
- Linkages among cases

Discovery output may take two forms. In *business discovery*, the analysis product is a visualization; for example, a *word cloud* is a way to visualize word count in a text. In *operational discovery*, the discovered pattern is an object passed to some other application; for example, a fraud detection application may use anomaly detection to identify unusual transactions and route them to an investigator for further analysis.

In the following sections, we describe a number of discovery use cases; these are distinguished from one another because they rely on fundamentally different techniques and tooling.

Text and Document Processing

Much of what we call *Big Data* consists of free text and documents, such as call center notes, medical records, blog posts, and Facebook comments. Working with text data poses two closely related but distinct problems. In some cases, analysts seek to supplement predictive models with features extracted from text; we call this the *text mining* problem. In other cases, the analytic goal is to work with whole documents to identify duplicates, detect plagiarism, monitor streams of incoming email, and so forth—we call this the *document analytics* problem. Sentiment analysis is a special case of document analytics, where the unit of text is a news report or social media comment.

Text mining requires specialized *text processing* tools enabling an analyst to correct spelling errors, reduce inflected or derived words to their stem, and suppress certain words (such as common conjunctions). After cleaning up the text, the analyst runs word count tooling that extracts words and phrases from text to create a word count matrix (where documents are rows and words are columns). The analyst then applies some form of dimension reduction (such as *singular value decomposition*) to the matrix. Next, the analyst uses visualization tools to produce a meaningful "picture" of the text, such as a word cloud. Additionally, the analyst can merge the reduced text feature matrix with other characteristics to build a predictive model.

When working with whole documents, the analyst may develop distance or similarity measures when the goal is to identify duplicates or detect plagiarism. Documents that score highly on similarity measures are good candidates for further review. Sentiment analysis requires highly sophisticated tools for natural language processing that are able to detect sarcasm or irony and classify comments as positive, negative, or neutral.

Given the volume of text and documents handled by large organizations, text and document processing tends to require highly scalable platforms. Hadoop is particularly well suited to this kind of analysis given its scalability, ability to support diverse data types, and low cost.

Segmentation

When the analytic goal is to group cases into homogeneous subgroups, or segments based on similarity across many variables, we call this a *segmentation* problem or use case. There are distinct methods available to analysts, called clustering techniques, to address this problem. Marketing researchers, for example, use clustering techniques to identify underlying market segments based on the richest possible information about each survey respondent. Clustering techniques can also play a role in predictive modeling where an analyst working with a very large universe of data may first run a multivariate segmentation to subdivide the universe and then develop separate predictive models for each segment.

There are currently more than 100 known methods for multivariate clustering. The most popular is k-means clustering.

Because clustering is a useful discovery tool, it is most effective when used with all of the available data. For this reason, clustering algorithms that run inside databases or Hadoop are particularly useful. Clustering algorithms are among the most highly developed projects within Apache Mahout, for example.

When the business expects to use the results of clustering for market segmentation, evaluation of the results is somewhat subjective, requiring close interplay between the analyst and business client. For this reason, clustering algorithms work ideally together with visualization capabilities enabling the business client to understand the characteristics of each cluster discovered by the algorithm.

Association

The analyst's goal in clustering is to group cases together based on common characteristics. Suppose, however, that you want to group items based on consumer choices rather than characteristics of the objects themselves; for example, you may want to understand which items consumers purchase together so you can recommend additional purchases or develop bundled products.

Association analysis refers to a set of techniques that identify the degree to which events tend to occur together. When applied to retail market basket analysis, for example, association learning tells you if there is an unusually high probability that consumers will purchase certain items together in the same shopping trip. (A famous example of this is the urban legend about beer and diapers.[1])

Association analysis requires item-level data; given the volume of retail transactions, this implies a need for scalable algorithms that can run on the data management platform. In some cases, the analyst can use a cluster sample (a sample of customers or shopping trips with all of the associated item transactions). However, some of the most interesting and useful associations may be rare and could be overlooked without examining the complete universe.

The best-known method for association analysis is the *a priori* algorithm, which can be difficult to scale. Recently developed alternatives that are better suited to Big Data include FP-Growth and Limited Pass algorithms (PCY, SON, and Toivonen's Algorithm).

Like clustering, association may require close collaboration between the analyst and the business client. The best tools for association analysis include a strong visualization and drill-down capability enabling the business user to understand discovered patterns.

Anomaly Detection

An anomaly is a case that is in some sense unusual. It may have an exceptionally large value on a single measure, such as a very large cash withdrawal by a bank depositor; alternatively, the case may demonstrate a pattern across multiple measures that do not fit the norm.

---

[1] Mark Whitehorn, "The Parable of the Beer and Diapers," *The Register*, August 15, 2006, http://www.theregister.co.uk/2006/08/15/beer_diapers/.

Depending on the business context, an outlier can indicate suspicious activity, a potential problem, an early indication of a new trend, or it may simply be a statistical anomaly. In any case, the outlier warrants further investigation.

The goal of anomaly detection is to flag such cases without overwhelming investigators with spurious "suspects." For convenience, we can classify outlier detection methods into three broad categories:

- General rule-based methods
- Adaptive rule-based methods
- Multivariate methods

Rule-based methods apply static rules to each case and flag exceptions. For example, a banking system will flag any cash deposit of $10,000 or more because such transactions trigger compliance action under U.S. banking law. Rule-based systems are easy to implement in operational systems and widely used across industries to support a variety of applications.

Although static rule-based systems work well when rules are clear (as is the case in many compliance applications), they are less useful when the anomalies you want to detect relate to human behavior. Human behavior tends to diverge widely so that what is exceptional for one person may be normal for another. A well-known credit card company advertises that it has "no pre-set limit" on its credit card; a customer who rarely uses the card but suddenly charges an expensive item may have to speak with someone in the call center to approve the transaction. The company uses an adaptive system that "learns" the usage patterns of individual customers and tailors rules accordingly.

Multivariate systems examine many measures and flag cases that do not fit established statistical patterns. A leading railroad company captures a large vector of data from scanners for each car that enters its yards; the company cannot physically inspect every car each time it enters the yard. Using multivariate outlier detection, though, the company can target individual cars whose behavior is outside the norm; the problem is unknown in advance, but an inspector can determine whether the car needs repair.

Anomalies do not imply bad behavior *per se*; an unusual transaction could mean that a fraudster has hijacked a credit card account, or it could mean that the legitimate cardholder wants to make a large purchase. Hence, organizations use outlier detection to prioritize cases for human inspection by fraud investigators, call center agents, or railroad car inspectors. These systems generally require "tuning" to ensure that human analysts are not overwhelmed by false positives. Outlier analytics measures the degree to which a particular case departs from "normal," but the analytics alone do not determine the precise cutoff point that distinguishes an outlier from all other cases; that must be determined by the business.

Organizations get the greatest benefit from outlier detection when the analytics run in real time, as transactions happen. Once a credit card issuer approves a transaction, it may be difficult or impossible to recover funds if the transaction is fraudulent.

Graph and Network Analysis

In mathematics, a graph is a structure depicting the relationship between objects. The graph consists of nodes representing objects and edges representing links, or relationships. There are established mathematical principles, called *graph theory,* used to produce insight about the behavior systems represented in graphs.

Mathematical graphs are a useful metaphor to describe systems (such as distributed computer networks), transportation networks, or the pages of a website. When you model a system in this manner, you can model such things as network traffic or click paths, and use this information to develop optimal routing plans or to predict a user's next click.

When you use a mathematical graph to model social systems, the result is a social network graph; such graphs are highly useful in a number of applications. Police investigations use social network analysis to identify organized crime rings; insurers use the method to detect fraud rings; and social media companies use the method to recommend new friends, predict traffic, and optimize advertising.

You can draw a simple social network on a whiteboard with a marker. The value in formal social network analysis is the ability to detect relationships in large populations; hence, applied graph analysis requires a scalable platform. Graph analysis is computationally complex and requires a specialized engine to support large problems.

Simulation

Simulation is an example of "big analytics" that does not depend on "Big Data." Most simulation problems do not rely on large data sets and do not benefit from tight integration with data platforms.

Grid computing provides an excellent platform to support simulation. In most cases, simulation is embarrassingly parallel; the fastest way to run an embarrassingly parallel simulation on 10,000 scenarios is to distribute it across 10,000 processors. Simulation is especially well suited to cloud computing because there is little or no data movement to constrain off-premises computing.

Simulation is also a good candidate for offload to a general-purpose graphics processing unit (GPGPU). Many investment and trading operations leverage GPGPUs for real-time options analysis based on complex market simulations; analysts report up to 750X speedup from implementing simulations in a GPU device.[2]

---

[2] Matthew Francis Dixon, Sabbir Khan, and Mohammed Zobair, "Accelerating Option Risk Analytics in R Using GPUs," November 25, 2013, http://papers.ssrn.com/sol3/papers.cfm?abstract_id=2359695.

Optimization

Mathematical optimization is a specialized field in analytics; it includes methods such as linear programming, quadratic programming, quadratically constrained programming, mixed-integer linear programming solver, mixed-integer quadratic programming, and mixed-integer quadratically constrained programming. While computationally complex, these methods place low demands on hardware I/O because even the largest optimization problems work with matrices that are comparatively small relative to other analytic applications. The most advanced optimization software generally runs on multi-threaded servers rather than in distributed computing environments.

Summary

In this chapter, we reviewed key analytic use cases. Use cases describe generic problems that analysts solve, together with the methods and technologies used to solve them. Understanding an organization's mix of analytic uses is key to building an enterprise architecture for analytics because no single technology supports all analytic uses.

In the following chapters, we discuss analytic methodology in more detail.

8

Predictive Analytics Methodology

Overview: The Modern Analytics Approach

The goal of predictive analytics is to predict something you do not know from facts that you *do* know. For example, you may know something about the characteristics of a home—its location, age, square footage, number of rooms, and so forth—but you do not know its market value. You want to know its market value so you can set an asking price. Similarly, you might want to predict whether a patient will develop a certain disease, the monthly minutes a cell phone customer will want to consume, or whether a borrower will make monthly payments on a loan. In each case, you want to use what you know to predict something you need to know.

Predictive analytics drives business value because reliable predictions lead to better decisions. If you can predict the market value of a home, you can set an asking price with confidence. Predicting disease, cell phone usage, and borrower payment behavior helps you make treatment decisions, price cell phone plans, and decide whether to approve a loan, respectively. In each case, there is real upside to an accurate prediction.

Techniques for predictive analytics detect relationships in historical data to predict future events or behavior. Predictive analytics is widely used across a range of business applications: predicting insurance claims, response to marketing campaigns, loan losses, purchasing behavior, product usage, customer attrition, and many other applications.

Suppose that treatment data shows that most patients diagnosed with the ABC disease respond well when treated with the XYZ medication, whereas some others develop side effects and die. You could decline to offer the XYZ medication to anyone due to the risk of side effects, but then most patients would continue to suffer with the disease. Alternatively, you could let patients make the decision, making sure that they sign legal releases indemnifying the medical providers from malpractice liability. However, the best approach would be to use analytics to predict the outcome of the treatment—the response measure—based on other information about the patient.

In Chapter 7, "Analytic Use Cases," we reviewed use cases for analytics; in this chapter, we review methodology for one use case, prediction (see Exhibit 8.1). The difference between a use case and a methodology is a matter of depth: A *methodology* explains and justifies a set of steps; it does not simply describe current practices. A methodology is prescriptive and forward-looking; it specifies an approach necessary to achieve a certain outcome.

There are many analytic methodologies—the two best known are the SAS SEMMA methodology and the CRISP-DM methodology (associated with SPSS). They are fine so far as they go, but each has its limitations. SEMMA, for example, assumes that the business problem is well defined and makes no reference to model deployment at all; model deployment, it seems, is someone else's job.

We believe that a Modern Analytics methodology should draw inspiration from agile software development and should fully exploit the capabilities of contemporary analytics tooling. For maximum effectiveness, the analyst and client should focus attention on the beginning and end of the process—on business definition and deployment. The technical activities that take place between definition and deployment, such as model training and validation, are important, but the key choices in these steps depend on how you define the problem.

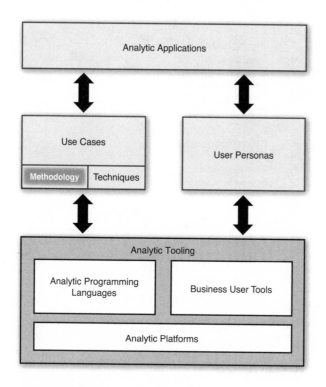

Exhibit 8.1   Modern Analytics Framework

In this chapter, we present an overview of the predictive analytics *process;* in the next chapter, we cover key methods and techniques. The predictive analytics process includes four primary steps or phases: business definition, data preparation, model development, and model deployment. Each phase includes a number of tasks. Exhibit 8.2 illustrates these steps and tasks.

The following sections describe and explain each phase and its supporting tasks.

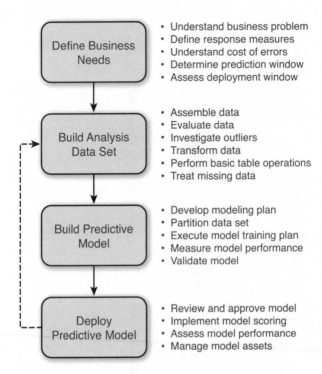

Exhibit 8.2   Predictive Analytics Methodology

Define Business Needs

It may seem obvious to you that an analysis project should begin with the end in mind and that the result should be a positive impact on the business. Obvious, perhaps, but all too often overlooked. When we speak with working analysts about projects they currently support, it is striking how often they do not know or are unable to articulate how the analysis they perform will affect the business.

Understand the Business Problem

Every analysis project, without exception, should begin with a clearly defined business goal, stated in terms that matter to project stakeholders:

- Improve the response rate on campaign ABC to at least $x\%$
- Reduce losses from fraudulent transactions by $y\%$
- Increase customer retention by $z\%$

Analysts frequently complain that organizations do not use the results of analysis. In other words, the analyst goes to great lengths to gather data, transform it, and perform analysis to construct a predictive model; at this point, the model goes into limbo, or is simply placed on a shelf and not used. We should see this outcome for what it is: a failure. In most cases, it is attributable to a lack of well-defined business impact. Unlike analysis itself, implementing predictive models is a cross-functional activity requiring collaboration among stakeholders, the analyst, and IT, and there are well-defined costs to the implementation of the project. If the business impact of a predictive model is undefined, it will be difficult to build a business case for implementation.

Define Response Measures

A response measure is something you do not know but want to predict. To drive value, the response measure should influence a decision or business process where the outcome of the decision affects the organization's key metrics.

Examples of response measures include such things as whether a prospect will respond to a targeted promotion, the likely sale price of a home, a browser's likely next click, or the point spread in a football game.

In most cases, the response measure represents a future event, which is why you do not know the outcome. For example, a credit card issuer may want to predict whether a customer will file for bankruptcy in the next year—an event that will happen in the future is inherently uncertain. You can check public records after the fact to see who has already filed for bankruptcy, but if the goal is to avoid losses on loans made to bankrupt customers, that information will be too late to be useful.

In some circumstances, the response measure represents a current or past event. For example, if bankruptcy records are unavailable in a jurisdiction for any reason, you can use a predictive model to estimate the likelihood that a customer has previously filed for bankruptcy based on other household information.

The time dimension of response measures should be explicit. Suppose that you want to predict whether a prospective borrower will default on a loan with an amortization period of ten years. Should you define the response measure to include defaults over the entire life of the loan or a shorter period? Long response windows are often more relevant to the business decision but require more history to validate. It is also more difficult to predict behavior over long periods than over short periods because there is a greater opportunity for external events to influence the behavior you seek to model.

For any given business application, there may be multiple responses to predict:

- A tax authority needs to determine which tax returns it should audit; audits are expensive, and the number of auditors is fixed. To maximize the yield per auditor, the authority should predict both the odds that a return understates income and the amount the authority can collect.

- A university seeks to maximize the return on its investment in an alumni donor campaign. To target different strategies appropriately, the university should predict both the likelihood that each alumnus will respond, and the amount each alumnus is likely to contribute.

For any given business problem, you might want to predict more than one response. For example, to maximize ROI on a targeted donor campaign, you might want to predict whether a prospect will respond to the offer and, if that prospect does respond, the amount he or she will donate.

Although techniques exist to model multiple responses in a single predictive model, most analysts prefer to break the problem into parts and build separate predictive models for each response measure. Disaggregating the problem in this manner enables the analyst to optimize the predictive models separately for each response effect, and provides business users more flexibility.

Consider also two groups of prospects: those with a low propensity to respond but high average donations, and those with a high propensity to respond but low average donations. The two segments have a similar overall expected value. However, disaggregating the response behavior and modeling each separately enables the client to distinguish between the two segments and apply different strategies.

Most prediction problems fall into two categories: classification and regression. In *classification,* the analyst seeks to predict a categorical event in the future; in most cases, this is a binary state. Hence, a customer either responds to a marketing campaign or does not respond; a debtor declares bankruptcy or does not do so. In *regression,* the analyst seeks to predict a continuous value, such as the number of cell phone minutes a customer will use, the amount a buyer will spend in a given period. Some techniques are appropriate for classification; others, for regression; and some support both. The analyst must understand the prediction problem to choose the correct technique.

Understand the Cost of Errors

Ideally, you would like a model to predict future events perfectly; in practice, you know that is impossible. If you abandon the notion that you can build a perfect predictive model, how much accuracy is "good enough"?

In general, a predictive model must improve the quality of your decisions by an amount sufficient to cover its development and deployment costs. Predictive models produce a positive economic benefit when the value at risk is high—in other words, when the cost of wrong decisions is large. This value at risk can be the product of many decisions about relatively small amounts, as in a credit card portfolio, or in a limited number of decisions about large amounts, as in a reinsurance portfolio.

If the value at risk is low, even a very good predictive model provides little or no economic benefit because the cost of making a wrong decision is minimal. Many organizations do not bother to build predictive models to target email campaigns because the incremental cost to send a message to an unresponsive customer is low. Of course, this means more spam in your inbox.

Assuming that the value at risk is sufficiently high to justify building a predictive model, the model must perform better than the best available naïve targeting rule. Analytic software vendors often use random selection as the baseline to demonstrate the strength of their algorithms. In practice, however, managers tend to have intuitive targeting rules for programs that are better than random; because these intuitive rules are inexpensive to develop—no analysts required—a predictive model must outperform them to justify its cost.

The overall accuracy of a predictive model is important, but you must also consider the composition of errors. A binary classification model can be right in two ways: It can accurately predict that an event will happen, or it can accurately predict that an event will not happen. The same model can be wrong in two ways: It can falsely predict that an event will happen, or it can falsely predict that an event will not happen.

Suppose that you develop a model that is designed to predict cardiac arrest among patients in an intensive care unit (ICU). If the model predicts cardiac arrest, the ICU staff will proactively apply treatments, in which case there is a much greater chance the patient will live. Otherwise, the staff will respond only if the patient actually goes into arrest; by then, it may be too late.

If the predictive model wrongly predicts cardiac arrest, that outcome is called a *false positive*; if the model predicts no cardiac arrest and the patient actually does arrest, the outcome is a *false negative*. In most real-world decisions, the costs of errors are asymmetric, which means that the costs of false positives are not the same as the costs of false negatives. In this case, the cost of a false positive is unnecessary treatments, whereas the cost of a false negative is the increased probability of patient death. In most medical decisions, the stakeholders would place greater weight on minimizing false negatives than on minimizing false positives.

Determine the Prediction Window

The required prediction window materially affects the design of an analysis project; it influences the choice of methods and choice of data. All predictions relate to future events, but business applications vary widely in requirements for how far in advance a prediction is useful. In retail, for example, a store shift planner may by interested only in expected store traffic for tomorrow or for the next several days; the merchandising executive has a longer time horizon and may be interested in store traffic for the next several months; and the site planner may be interested in forecasting traffic for several years.

As a rule, model precision declines as the prediction window lengthens; in other words, it is much easier to predict store traffic tomorrow than it is to predict store traffic three years from now. There are two main reasons for this. First, as the prediction window expands, the odds of a disruptive event increase. For example, if a natural disaster hits the neighborhood in which your store is located, the volume of store traffic will change. Second, over time, random errors accumulate and can cause significant drift in a prediction.

The required prediction window also affects the data you will use as predictors in your analysis. Keeping with the retail example, suppose that you want to predict traffic for one store one day in advance. The chances are very good that a time series analysis based on volatile measures, such as daily traffic for the past several days, will work well. On the other hand, if you seek to forecast store traffic for the next three years, you may have to include data about fundamental factors, such as local housing construction, household formation, or changes in household income, as well as possible changes to the competitive landscape.

Assess the Deployment Environment

Deployment is an organic part of the analytics process, and the analyst must understand a predictive model's deployment environment before beginning work on a predictive modeling project.

Organizations deploy predictive models in one of two ways: batch or transaction. In batch prediction, a scoring engine computes record-level predictions for a group of entities and stores the results in a repository; consuming applications retrieve the prediction from the repository and use it as needed. In transactional deployment, the scoring engine computes predictions for individual records on request by a consuming application, which uses the prediction immediately. Transactional or real-time scoring is vital for applications that require little or no score latency; however, they are more expensive to implement, and applications do not necessarily require minimal latency.

The analyst must know what data is available to an application in the deployment environment. This is an important point because analysts tend to work in "sandbox" environments where it is relatively easy to procure data and merge it into an analytic data set. In a production environment, there may be operational or legal constraints that prevent use of the data or make it very expensive to use.

It can be useful, from a strategic perspective, to use data in a predictive model that is currently unavailable in the deployment environment if the intent is to use analytics to determine what data has the most value to the business. In this case, however, the organization should plan for an extended implementation period.

The deployment environment also influences the analyst's choice of methods. Some methods, such as linear regression or decision trees, produce predictive models in a form that is easy to implement in SQL-based systems. Other methods, such as support vector machines or neural networks, are relatively hard to implement. Some predictive analytics software packages support model export in a variety of formats; however, the deployment environment may or may not support the formats supported by the analytics package, and the analytics package may not support model export for all analytic techniques.

Build the Analysis Data Set

Working data scientists spend most[1] of their time preparing data for analysis, a process that includes data collection, assessment, and transformation. Building an analysis data set is the first "hands-on" step in predictive analytics; analysts understand that this task is essential for effective model building, and they invest as much time as needed to get it right.

Since data preparation tasks account for a large portion of total cycle time, they present the opportunity for process improvement and streamlining.

---

[1] http://blogs.hbr.org/2014/04/the-sexiest-job-of-the-21st-century-is-tedious-and-that-needs-to-change/.

Assemble the Data

In a perfect world, analysts simply connect analytic tools to a high-performance enterprise repository that offers a single version of the truth. The real world of enterprise analytics differs from the vision in a number of respects: Data lives in diverse source systems inside and outside the organization; data cleanliness, integrity, and organization run the gamut from "messy" to "clean, well-organized, and well-documented." Although enterprises have made great strides in data warehousing and master data management, few are able to keep up with growing volumes and complexity of data. Because analysts work for internal clients who have immediate business needs, they are often required to perform work well ahead of the IT organization.

Analysts report that they spend a great deal of time simply collecting and consolidating data. Most of this time goes into investigating potential sources, understanding data capture, and procuring documentation and permission to use the data. Physically moving the data to an analytic "sandbox" tends to take relatively little time.

Evaluate the Data

Upon receipt of a data file, the analyst first determines if the data format is compatible with the analytic software. This is not always the case; there are thousands of possible file formats, although analytic software tools tend to support a limited number. If the analyst can read the data, the next step is to perform tests to verify that the data conforms to available documentation. (If there is no documentation, the analyst will spend time "guessing" the format and content of the file.)

If the data file is readable, the analyst will read the entire file (or a sample if the file is very large) and perform some basic checks on the data. For tabular data, these checks include

- Determine the presence (or absence) of a key value if it will be necessary to join to other tables.

- Ensure that each field is populated. The field does not need to be populated for every record, but fields that are empty for all rows can be dropped from the analysis.

- Check for variance in the field. Fields populated with the same value for each row can be dropped from the analysis.

- Determine the type of data in the field: floating-point, integer, character, date, or another data type. (Data types are platform-specific.)

- Determine whether there is a field in the data file corresponding to the response measure of interest for the project.

The minimum requirement for predictive modeling is a data set consisting of a response measure that corresponds with the behavior of interest to the business, plus at least one candidate predictor variable; response and predictor variables must have positive variance. In most cases, the analyst will need to perform additional work to create the appropriate measures. The next section covers these tasks.

Investigate Outliers

Cases with extreme values, or outliers, can exercise an unwarranted influence on the modeling process. In extreme cases, they can make it difficult to fit a good model at all. Nevertheless, the analyst cannot simply discard outliers arbitrarily; an insurance analyst cannot simply discard losses from Hurricane Katrina from a data set simply because they are extreme.

The analyst should investigate outliers to determine whether they are an artifact of the data collection process. For example, an analyst working with supermarket point of sale data discovered a few accounts with extraordinarily large spending amounts. Upon investigation, he found that these "extreme" customers were store cashiers swiping their own cards so that shoppers with no loyalty card would receive in-store discounts.

In another example, an analyst working with data from a leasing company found that in one market there appeared to be an unusually large number of approved loan applications that customers did not subsequently activate and use. The analyst and clients developed a number of hypotheses to "explain" the observed behavior. Upon investigation, however, the analyst discovered that system administrators had cycled a large volume of test applications through the system without distinguishing them from real customer applications.

Transform the Data

Details of data transformation required before modeling begins depend on the condition of the data and the requirements of the project. Because these requirements vary for every project, it is impossible to generalize about the details of data transformation, but it is possible to review the reasons for data transformation as well as generic types of operations.

There are two principal reasons analysts transform the data they work with. The first reason is that the source data does not conform to the business rules for the application. In principle, the organization should implement processes in the back end of a data warehouse to ensure data complies with business rules; this ensures consistent application across the enterprise. Unfortunately, analysts often must work ahead of the data warehousing organization and use data that is not yet part of an enterprise data warehouse.

There is also the special case of analysts who apply business rules that differ from the enterprise business rules because doing so produces favorable results for the internal client. This practice is illogical and counterproductive from the enterprise's perspective, but is surprisingly prevalent.

The second reason analysts transform data is to improve the accuracy and precision of the predictive models they build. These transformations include simple mathematical transformations (such as power functions or log transforms), "binning" numeric variables, recoding categorical variables as well as more complex operations such as missing value treatment or mining text to extract features. Transformations may be required for some techniques but not others, and analytic software packages often handle required transforms automatically; hence, simpler operations belong to the model training step outlined later in this chapter.

Transforming the data extensively increases model precision and accuracy when the analyst validates the model. However, the most important question the analyst should ask is whether the required transforms are possible to implement in the deployment environment. "Munging" the data in an analytic sandbox does not improve the in-market performance of a predictive model unless the data in the deployment environment can be "munged" using the same transformations.

Perform Basic Table Operations

Analytic software tools generally require all data (response measures and predictors) to be loaded into a single table. Unless all of the required data is already in a single table, the analyst must perform table operations to build the analytic data set. These operations include

- Join tables
- Append tables
- Select rows
- Drop rows

- Add a column and populate with a calculated field
- Drop columns
- Group by

High-performance SQL engines are generally more efficient than analytic software for table operations. Analysts should leverage these tools for basic data preparation wherever possible.

Treat Missing Data

Data can be missing from a data set for several reasons. Data can be logically missing: for example, when a data table includes fields to record a customer's data service usage, but the customer does not subscribe to a data service. In other cases, data is missing because the source system uses an implicit zero coding (zeros are represented as blanks). Data can also be missing due to an artifact of the data capture process; for example, if a customer declines to answer an income question, the field may be blank.

Many statistical packages require a value in each cell of the working data table and will drop any row from the table that does not have a value for each column. As a result, analysts use a number of tools to infer values for missing data using methods ranging from simple mean substitution to complex nearest neighbor methods.

Treatments for missing data do not add information value to the data; they simply make it possible to use certain techniques that cannot handle missing data. Because missing data is rarely a random phenomenon, analysts should use inference techniques only with great care, after the analyst understands why the data is missing in the first place.

As with other transformations, the analyst should also ask whether it is possible to "fix" missing data in the deployment environment and at what cost. Rather than "fixing" missing data in the analytic data set, the better practice may be to use a technique that can work with missing data, such as decision trees (covered in the next chapter).

Build the Predictive Model

Although analysts often state strong preferences for one technique over another, it is impossible to know in advance which technique will produce the best predictive model for a given problem with a specific data set. The technique that produces the best predictive model for a given problem cannot be determined in advance; the analyst must run experiments to determine the best model. Modern high-performance analysis platforms enable analysts to run a large number of experiments; moreover, analytic software packages frequently include scripting capabilities so the analyst can specify and run experiments in batch.

Develop Modeling Plan

Although modern analytic platforms enable analysts to run brute force searches for the best model, for most problems, the number of experiments can be impossibly large. Modeling techniques provide analysts with a wide range of parameters, any one of which can make a material difference in the quality of the model. Moreover, each new predictor variable added to the analytic data set creates multiple new ways to specify a model; there is the main effect of the new predictor to consider, as well as multiple mathematical transformations of the model, plus interaction effects between the new predictor and all existing predictors.

The analyst can reduce the experimental search space in several ways. First, the characteristics of the response variable and predictors narrow the range of feasible analytic techniques, as shown in Exhibit 8.3.

Exhibit 8.3 Methods by Variable Characteristics

Technique	Response Measure	Predictors
Linear Regression	Continuous	Continuous
Generalized Linear Models	Depends on Distribution	Continuous
Generalized Additive Models	Depends on Distribution	Continuous
Logistic Regression	Categorical or Ordinal	Continuous
Survival Analysis	Time to Event	Continuous
Decision Trees		
CHAID	Categorical	Categorical
Classification and Regression Trees	Continuous or Categorical	Continuous or Categorical
ID3	Categorical	Categorical
C4.5/C5.0	Continuous or Categorical	Continuous or Categorical
Naïve Bayes	Categorical	Categorical
Neural Networks	Continuous or Categorical	Continuous (Standardized)

Second, the analyst can narrow the range of experiments by measuring the information value of each available predictor variable and dropping variables with little or no value from further analysis. By starting with regularized or stepwise versions of a modeling technique, the analyst produces a preliminary model that includes only those variables with positive information value. Many analytic software packages include built-in feature selection algorithms. The analyst can also leverage open feature selection tools, such as the Feature Selection Toolbox, the TOOLDIAG Pattern Recognition Toolbox, or the RRF package in R for regularized random forests.

Partition the Data Set

Splitting, or partitioning, the analytic data set should be the last step prior to actual model training. Analysts disagree about the appropriate number and size of the partitions, but there is broad consensus on several points.

First, the analyst should use random sampling to create all partitions. Simple sampling, systematic sampling, stratified sampling, and cluster sampling are all acceptable as long as the analyst uses a random process.

Second, the analyst should select one data set at random and hold it out from the model training process. This data set should be large enough that the analyst and client can draw meaningful conclusions about the performance of the model applied to production data.

Depending on the specific analytic methods used, the analyst may further subdivide remaining records into Training and Pruning data sets. Some methods, such as Classification and Regression Trees, incorporate a native capability to train on one data set and prune on another data set.

When working with a very large number of records, the analyst can speed up experimentation by splitting the training data set into equal replicates and then running a range of model specifications on a single replicate. The analyst can discard poorly performing methods after running on the first replicate and then expand the sample size; alternatively, the analyst can explicitly measure how well the model performs as the sample size expands.

Execute the Model Training Plan

In this task, the analyst performs the technical steps needed to execute the model-training plan. The detailed technical steps vary with the technique used and the software implementation of the technique. Ideally, however, the analyst has automated this task using native automation capabilities in the analytic software or through custom scripting. Because the number of individual-model runs in an effective model-training plan may be large, the analyst should avoid manual execution as much as possible.

Measure Model Performance

When you run a large number of models, you need an objective way to measure the performance of each model, so you can rank-order candidates and select the best. Without an objective measure of model performance, the analyst and client must rely on manual assessment of each model, which necessarily limits the number of possible experiments.

There are many possible ways to measure model performance. The "acid test" measure of a model is its business impact, but it is rarely possible to measure this impact effectively within the modeling context, so analysts generally rely on proxy measures. Four general criteria govern the choice of metric:

- Measures should generalize across specific modeling methods and techniques.
- Measures should reflect model performance with an independent sample.
- Measures should reflect model performance across a broad range of data.
- Measures should be interpretable by analyst and client alike.

Individual modeling techniques, such as linear regression or logistic regression, produce goodness-of-fit measures, such as the R-Squared and the Wald Statistic. Unfortunately, these measures do not generalize across methods, so they are not acceptable when the analyst plans to test a broad range of methods.

Available measures generally fall into three groups:

- Measures suitable for categorical response measures (classification)

- Measures suitable for continuous response measures (regression)

- Measures that are suitable for either classification or regression

For classification problems, simple overall classification accuracy is easy to compute and understand. Presented with a contingency table ("confusion matrix"), this measure is highly interpretable. Exhibit 8.4 shows an example.

Exhibit 8.4   Confusion Matrix

		Actual Behavior	
Predicted Behavior	**Response**	**No Response**	**Total**
Response	312	4,688	**5,000**
No Response	224	44,776	**45,000**
Total	**536**	**49,464**	**50,000**

Overall Accuracy: (312 + 44776)/50,000 = **90%**

Overall classification accuracy does not distinguish between false positives and false negatives; in real-world analytics, however, payoff matrices are always asymmetrical, and the two types of error have different costs. One predictive model may demonstrate better overall accuracy than another model, but unless you understand the distribution of false positives and false negatives, you may not choose the best model. For that, you need to consider three additional measures.

Sensitivity (correctly classified positives divided by total positives) measures how well the model minimizes false negatives; *specificity* (correctly classified negatives divided by total negatives) measures how well the model minimizes false positives. Model *precision* (correctly classified positives divided by total predicted positives) measures the incidence of errors. Exhibit 8.5 shows these statistics added to the previous table.

Exhibit 8.5   Confusion Matrix

		Actual Behavior	
Predicted Behavior	**Response**	**No Response**	**Total**
Response	312	4,688	**5,000**
No Response	224	44,776	**45,000**
Total	**536**	**49,464**	**50,000**

Accuracy: (312 + 44776)/50,000 = **90%**

Sensitivity: 312/536 = **58%**

Specificity: 44776/49464 = **90%**

Suppose that you build a model designed to predict whether a patient diagnosed with a particular disease will respond to a medical treatment; there is no other treatment, so "no treatment" means the patient dies. Most medical practitioners would want to minimize false negatives—the number of patients who would have responded to the treatment that the model classifies as "do not treat." In this case, the analyst and client would agree to a minimum required specificity for the model, or they would choose the model with the greatest specificity.

Alternatively, suppose the purpose of the model is to optimize the response rate on a marketing campaign. The marketing program manager does not care about false negatives—customers not targeted by the campaign who would have responded—because campaign response rates are very visible but opportunity costs are not. This client should specify a minimum level of precision or choose the model that produces the highest precision.

For most modeling methods, the raw output of the model is a score reflecting the odds of membership in a class or (in the case of tree-based methods) an assignment to one of many leaf nodes in a tree. Hence, actual classification requires two steps: The analyst first generates raw output and then uses a cutoff or assignment rule (the discrimination threshold) to produce the desired binary classification. The measures cited previously (accuracy, sensitivity, specificity, and precision) reflect the result of this two-step process.

The Receiver Operating Characteristic (ROC) curve (see the example in Exhibit 8.6) graphically shows the sensitivity and specificity of a model for various levels of the discrimination thresholds. A model whose curve is closest to the upper-left corner across all values is unambiguously the best model. The area under the ROC curve (ROC AUC) statistic reduces the graphic representation to a single measure.

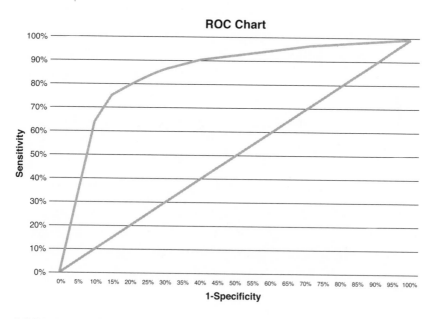

Exhibit 8.6   ROC Chart

For continuous response measures, the number of available measures is more limited; the most common measure is the root mean square error (RMSE). To develop this measure, the analyst uses a model to compute predicted and residual values for each observation in a test sample—residual values are the difference between the predicted and actual value. The analyst then squares the residual, computes the mean residual for the sample, and takes the square root of the mean.

The most widely used model quality measure that is appropriate for both classification and regression is the Akaike information criterion (AIC). The AIC estimates the degree of separation between a model's likelihood function and the (unknown) true likelihood function; a lower AIC implies a better model. The AIC formula penalizes complexity, so that if two models perform equally well at prediction, the simpler model will produce a better AIC metric.

The AIC measure is similar to the Bayesian information criterion (BIC). The BIC is an estimate of a posterior probability of a model being true; as with the AIC, a lower value implies a better model. Compared to the AIC, however, the BIC imposes a greater penalty on model complexity.

In most cases, the AIC and BIC produce the same rank ordering for a group of models, but there are a few exceptions. Because the BIC penalizes complexity more heavily than the AIC, a model that is significantly more complex but only slightly better at prediction may have a higher ranking when the analyst uses the AIC measure.

Neither the AIC nor the BIC has an absolute meaning; these criteria are useful for rank ordering models but do not address whether a model is "good enough" to place into production.

Validate the Model

In the course of an analytics project, an analyst may produce hundreds of candidate models. Validation serves two purposes. First, it helps the analyst detect overlearning, a situation that occurs when an algorithm learns the characteristics of the training data too well but does not generalize to the population. Second, validation helps the analyst rank the candidate models from best to worst to identify the best choice for the business.

Analysts distinguish between several kinds of validation:

- N-fold cross-validation
- Split-sample validation
- Out-of-time sample validation

N-fold cross-validation is a method that enables the analyst to leverage a small sample by subsampling available data into multiple overlapping replicates and validating the model separately against each replicate. This is a reasonable method to use when data is very expensive (clinical trials, for example) but is unnecessary for Big Data.

In split-sample validation, the analyst splits the available data into two samples, using one to train models and the other to validate models. Some analytical tools have a built-in capability to specify training and validation data sets so that the analyst can combine the two steps.

An out-of-time sample may be required for secondary validation before model deployment. The analyst draws a completely independent sample at a different point in time from the original sample used for model training and validation. This is a check to ensure that estimates of model accuracy and precision are stable.

Deploy the Predictive Model

Until the organization deploys a predictive model, it delivers no value. In some organizations, deployment planning begins when modeling ends; this often leads to considerable delay and long deployment cycles. In the worst case, the result is a failed project, which is surprisingly frequent. In the most recent Rexer survey of working analysts, only 16%[2] said that their organizations "always" implement results of analysis.

Deployment planning should begin before modeling starts. The analyst must understand technical, organizational, and legal constraints before starting work on the model. When planning begins early, the IT organization can perform some tasks in parallel with model development to reduce total cycle time.

---

[2] Attribute to Rexer, 2013.

Review and Approve the Predictive Model

In many organizations, the first step toward deployment is a formal review and approval of the predictive model. This governance step serves several purposes: First, it ensures that the model complies with relevant laws and regulations governing the use of personal information; second, it provides an opportunity for peer review of the model and the methods used to build the model. Finally, formal approval serves as a budgetary control over resources required to productionize the model.

The approval process actually begins before analysis begins. It makes little sense to begin a predictive modeling project without committed deployment resources. Analysts and clients should fully understand pertinent legal constraints on the use of data before assembling the data set; if legal and compliance review mandates removal of a single predictor from a model, the analyst will have to re-estimate the entire model.

If the analyst and client assessed the deployment environment adequately in the first phase of the project, there should be no surprises in the review step. If the model uses data not present in the production environment, the organization will need to invest in feeds or Extract/Transform/Load (ETL) processes to implement the model. This will increase project cycle time.

Implement Model Scoring

Organizations implement model scoring either as batch processes or as transactional operations, and they either use native prediction within the analytics platform or transfer the model to a production application, as shown in Exhibit 8.7.

Exhibit 8.7   Matrix of Scoring Options

Scoring Engine	Scoring Mode	Model Integration	Data Movement	Score Latency
Model Building Environment	Batch	N/A	Extensive	High
	Transaction (*)		Minimal (**)	Low
In-Database	Batch	PMML or Custom Code	No	Medium
	Transaction (*)		Minimal (**)	Low
Application	Transaction		Minimal (**)	Low
Hybrid (Staged Scores)	Batch		Low (***)	Medium

(*) Requires scoring API and real-time integration

(**) Features for single record only

(***) Scores only

The detailed steps for implementation vary with the organization and deployment mode. We discuss the technical aspects in Chapter 10, "Analytic Platforms"; here, we offer some general observations from the methodological perspective.

Model deployment in a production application necessarily entails working across departments or business units. In most businesses, the IT organization manages production applications; these applications may have other business stakeholders who must review and approve the predictive model before deployment. This is another reason it is critical to define and understand the deployment environment before analysis begins.

Model deployment in the analytics application requires less coordination across the organization (which is why the practice persists) but is highly inefficient, because it poses extra demands on the analytics team. As a rule, analytic software vendors do not design or build software to support production-level performance and security requirements. Moreover, analytic teams rarely have the procedures or disciplines in place to support production operations.

Batch scoring is appropriate for high-latency analytics that consume infrequently updated data. When all of the predictors share the same update cycle, the most efficient way to implement the scoring process is to embed it in the ETL process that updates the repository where scores will be stored. Otherwise, an in-database procedure triggered by updates to any predictor will be most efficient.

Transactional scoring is the best model for low-latency analytics where the business requires using the freshest possible data. Transactional scoring is *required* when the predictive model consumes in-session data, such as data input by a website user or call center agent. For real-time transactional scoring, organizations generally use specialized applications designed for low latency.

Regardless of the deployment mode, the analyst is responsible for ensuring that the production-scoring model accurately reproduces the approved predictive model. In some cases, the analyst actually writes the scoring code; more often, the analyst writes a specification and then participates in acceptance testing for the application.

We discuss technical aspects of model integration in Chapter 10. Although the technology exists today to eliminate manual programming to produce scoring models, many organizations lack the required alignment of data flows and schemas to use this technology effectively. Consequently, manual programming remains a bottleneck in the model deployment cycle for many organizations.

Assess Model Performance

The validation testing performed at the end of the model development step provides the business with confidence that the model will be effective when deployed in production. It does not prove the value of the model, which you can determine only after you deploy the model.

In a perfect world, predictive models would perform as well in production as they do in validation testing; in the real world, models may underperform for a number of reasons. The most serious is simply poor execution: The analyst built an analytic data set that did not represent the population, did not control for overlearning, or transformed the data in irreproducible ways. However, even competently executed predictive models can "drift" over time because the underlying behavior changes. Consumer attitudes and tastes may change; a model that once predicted purchase propensity no longer works as well as it did when first deployed.

The organization must track and monitor the performance of deployed models. It can do this in two principal ways. The simplest method is to capture scoring history, analyze the distribution of scores on a regular cycle, and match the observed distribution with the distribution of scores to the original model validation. If the model validation scores followed a normal distribution, for example, you should expect the production scores to follow a normal distribution also. If the production scores do not align with the model validation scores, the underlying process may be changing in ways that could affect model performance. In a credit scoring application, for example, if the production scores show a skew toward higher risk, the business may have adopted practices leading to adverse selection.

Drifting score distribution does not mean the model no longer works, but it should trigger further investigation. To assess model performance, the analyst performs a validation study by matching scores to actual behavior. In practice, this can take as much time and effort as rebuilding the model from scratch. As modern technology automates the modeling process, many organizations skip the validation study entirely and simply rebuild production models on a regular cycle.

Manage Model Assets

A predictive model is an asset that the organization must manage. The scope of this asset management challenge grows as the organization expands its investment in analytics.

At the most basic level, model management is simply a cataloging operation: building and maintaining a record of each model asset in a repository suitable for browsing and searching. At minimum, this reduces duplicated effort; a project requested by one business unit may have requirements that closely match those of an existing asset. Ideally, a catalog includes information about response and predictor variables and supporting source data. This enables the organization to identify data dependencies and impacted models when it removes a data source from service.

At a higher level, the model management repository retains information about the model life cycle. This includes key artifacts from model development and validation, such as expected model score distributions, plus periodic updates with data from production.

Updating the model repository is the final task in the predictive modeling workflow.

Summary

In this chapter, we reviewed what we call the Modern Analytics methodology for predictive analytics. It should be clear that a methodology for advanced analytics in the contemporary enterprise is not simply a set of technical instructions for hacking with data. There are necessary organizational steps to ensure that predictive models accomplish organization goals and do not expose the business to undue legal or regulatory risk.

In the next chapter, we review widely used techniques for predictive analytics.

9

End-User Analytics

Overview

In this chapter, we cover leading tools used by working analysts to perform the tasks described in the previous three chapters (see Exhibit 9.1). First, we describe the most common analyst user personas—general categories of users with common needs and preferences. Next, we cover the most widely used analytic programming languages. We close the chapter with a brief description of some widely used analysis tools with a business user interface.

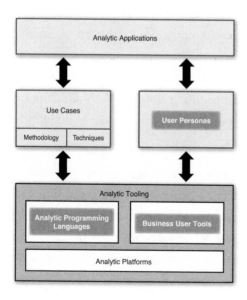

Exhibit 9.1   Modern Analytics Framework

Organizations seeking to gain broad acceptance for analytics must recognize divergent user needs. Many users in the modern enterprise require easy-to-use code-free user interfaces. However, easy-to-use tools may lack key features required for the most sophisticated analysis, or for custom analytics.

To achieve the broadest possible impact, focus on three critical success factors:

- **Focus on data infrastructure**—Sophisticated analysts spend a great deal of time on "data wrangling": acquiring, transforming, and cleaning up raw data. Business users cannot afford to do that; these users require an easily accessible source of clean, reliable data.

- **Enable collaboration**—Sophisticated users play a key role developing, testing, and validating analytical applications; they make sure the underlying math is right. Business user tools should consume and leverage advanced analytics developed by sophisticated analysts.

- **Tailor analytics to business processes**—Analytics are most productive when they directly affect a business process. Users do not need to perform "business analysis"; they need to perform credit analysis, workforce analysis, or some other task using your data and business rules. Tools should support custom analytic applications targeted to specific business processes, roles, and tasks.

For maximum business impact, develop an approach to analytics that supports the variety of user communities in your organization, from novice to expert. Build a high-performance data platform with clean and accessible data, enable collaboration among your user communities, and tailor analytics to support your business processes. These are the keys to building a smarter organization.

User Personas

In most organizations, there are four distinct user personas for analytics:

- Power Analysts
- Data Scientists
- Business Analysts
- Analytics Consumers

While these user personas do not capture all analytic requirements, they provide a framework to help you understand the needs of actual users. We describe each user persona in the sections that follow.

Power Analyst

Power analysts see advanced analytics as a full-time job and hold positions such as statistician, actuary, or risk analyst. They tend to work on teams in organizations that have significant investments in analytics or as consultants and developers in organizations that provide analytic services. Power analysts understand conventional statistics and machine learning, and have considerable working experience in applied analytics.

Power analysts prefer to work in an analytic programming language such as Legacy SAS or R. They have enough training and working experience with the language to be productive, and consider analytic programming languages to be more flexible and powerful than analytic software packages with GUI interfaces. They do not need analytics to be "easy" and may look down on those who do.

The "right" analytic method is extremely important to power analysts; they tend to be more concerned with using the "correct" methodology than with actual differences in business results achieved with different methods. This means, for example, if a particular analytic problem calls for a specific method or class of methods, such as survival analysis, power analysts will go to great lengths to use this method even if the improvement to predictive accuracy is very small.

In practice, because working power analysts tend to work with highly diverse problems and cannot always predict the nature of the problems they will need to address, they place a premium on being able to use a wide variety of analytic methods and techniques. The need for a particular method or technique may be rare, but power analysts want to be able to use it if the need arises.

Because data preparation is critical to successful predictive analytics, power analysts need to be able to understand and control the data they work with. This does not mean that power analysts want to manage the data or perform ETL tasks; it means that they need the data management processes to be transparent and responsive. In organizations where IT does not place a premium on supporting predictive analytics, power analysts will take over data management and ETL to meet their own needs, but this is not necessarily the working model they prefer.

The work product of power analysts may be a management report of some kind showing the results of an analysis, a predictive model specification to be recoded for production, a predictive model object (such as a PMML document), or an actual executable scoring function written in a programming language such as Java or C. Power analysts do not want to be heavily involved in production deployment or routing model scoring, although they may be forced into this role if the organization has not invested in tooling for model score deployment.

Power analysts are highly engaged in the specific brand, release, and version of analytic software. In organizations where the analytics team has significant influence, they play a decisive role in selecting analytic software. They also want control over the technical infrastructure supporting the analytic software, although they tend to be indifferent about specific brands of hardware, databases, storage, and so forth.

Data Scientist

Data scientists are similar in many respects to power analysts. Both roles share a lack of interest in easy-to-use tooling, and a desire to engage at a granular level with the data.

The principal differences between data scientists and power analysts relate to background, training, and approach. On one hand, power analysts tend to understand statistical methods, bring a statistical orientation to analytics, and tend to prefer working with higher-level languages with built-in analytic syntax. Data scientists, on the other hand, tend to come from a machine learning, engineering, or computer science background. Consequently, they tend to prefer working with programming languages such as C, Java, or Python and tend to be much better equipped to work with SQL and MapReduce. They have working experience with Hadoop, and this may be their preferred working environment.

Data scientists' machine learning roots influence their methods, techniques, and approach, which affect their requirements for analytic tooling. The machine learning discipline tends to focus less on choosing the "right" analytic method and places the focus on results of the predictive analytics process, including the predictive power of the model produced by the process. Hence, they are much more open to various forms of brute force learning, and choose methods that may be difficult to defend within the statistical paradigm but demonstrate good results.

Data scientists tend to have low regard for existing analytic software vendors, especially those like SAS and IBM that cater to business customers by soft-peddling technical details; instead, they tend to prefer open source tooling. They seek the best "technical" solution, one with sufficient flexibility to support innovation. Data scientists tend to engage directly in the process of "productionizing" their analytic findings; power analysts, in contrast, tend to prefer an entirely hands-off role in the process.

Business Analyst

Business analysts use analytics within the context of a role in the organization where analytics is important but not the exclusive responsibility. They hold a range of titles, such as loan officer, marketing analyst, or merchandising specialist.

Business analysts are familiar with analytics and may have some training and experience. Nevertheless, they prefer an easy-to-use interface and software such as SAS Enterprise Guide, SAS Enterprise Miner, SPSS Statistics, or a range of other products.

Although power analysts are very concerned with choosing the "right" method for the problem, business analysts tend to prefer a simpler approach. For example, they may be familiar with regression analysis, but they are unlikely to be interested in all of the various kinds of regression and the details of how regression models are calculated. They value "wizard" tooling that guides the selection of methods and techniques within a problem-solving framework.

Business analysts may be aware that data is important to the success of analytics but do not want to deal with it directly. Instead, business analysts prefer to work with data that is certified correct by others in the organization. Face validity matters to business analysts; data should be internally consistent and align with the analyst's understanding of the business.

In most cases, the work product of a business analyst is a report summarizing the results of an analysis. The work product may also be a decision of some kind, such as the volume of merchandise to a complex loan decision. Business analysts rarely produce predictive models for production deployment because their working methods tend to lack the rigor and exhaustiveness of power analysts.

Business analysts value good, customer-friendly technical support and tend to prefer using software from vendors with demonstrated credibility in analytics.

Analytics Consumers

Analytics consumers are fully focused on business questions and issues and do not engage directly in the production of analytics; instead, they use the results of analytics in the form of automated decisions, forecasts, and other forms of intelligence that are embedded into the business processes in which they engage.

Analytics consumers are not necessarily top management or any other specific level in the organization; they are simply not professionally engaged in the "sausage-making" of forecasts, automated decisions, and so forth.

Although analytic consumers may not engage with mathematical computations, they are concerned with the overall utility, performance, and reliability of the systems they use. For example, a customer service rep in a credit card call center may not be concerned with the analytic method used to determine a decision but will be very concerned if the system takes a long time to reach a decision. The rep may also object if the system does not provide reasonable explanations when it declines a credit request or appears to decline too many customers who seem to be good risks.

Because the range of possible ways that analytics can positively affect business processes is large and growing rapidly, and because embedded analytics have few barriers to use, this group of users has the greatest growth potential.

Analytic Programming Languages

We classify a programming language as an "analytic" language if its primary users are analysts and the language has native high-level functions required by analysts. It is possible to use general-purpose languages (such as Java or Python), for advanced analytics through custom coding or external analytics libraries. There is growing interest among data scientists to use Python for machine learning, although at this time it is still less widely used for analytics than the three languages described next.

The R Project

The R Project is an object-oriented open source programming language for statistics and advanced analytics. R's popularity for advanced analytics is rapidly growing; 70% of respondents surveyed in the 2013 Rexer Data Mining Survey[1] said they use R more than any other analytics platform.

R is an integrated suite of software supporting:

- Data handling and storage
- Operators for calculations on arrays and matrices
- Tools for data analysis
- Graphics facilities
- Programming functions such as input and output, conditionals, loops, and recursive operations

The R Core Development Team leads ongoing enhancement to the core software environment, while R users in the community contribute packages to support specific tasks. As of March 2013, there

---

[1] Rexer Analytics, "2013 Data Miner Survey," http://www.rexeranalytics.com/Data-Miner-Survey-Results-2013.html.

were 6,275 R packages in all major repositories worldwide,[2] of which 4,315 were in the Comprehensive R Archive Network (CRAN), the most widely used R library; as of the end of 2013, the CRAN package count exceeded 5,000. Exhibit 9.2 illustrates this explosive growth in capabilities.

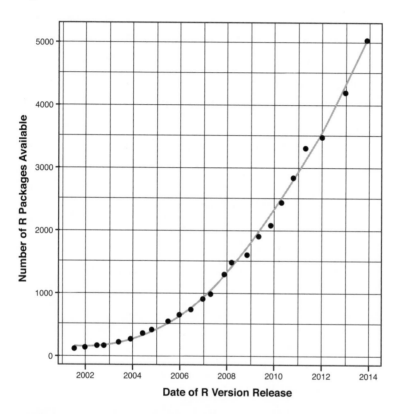

Exhibit 9.2   Number of CRAN Packages

Muenchen, Robert A.: The Popularity of Data Analysis Software, http://r4stats.com/articles/popularity

The R distribution includes 14 base packages that support basic statistics, graphics, and valuable utilities. Users may selectively add

---

[2] Robert A. Muenchen, "R's 2012 Growth in Capability Exceeds SAS' All Time Total," March 19, 2013, http://r4stats.com/2013/03/19/r-2012-growth-exceeds-sas-all-time-total/.

packages from CRAN or other libraries. Due to the broad developer community and low barriers to contribution, the breadth of functionality available in R far exceeds that of commercial analytic software.

Although the R Core Development Team takes responsibility for the R foundation software, individual package developers are responsible for the quality of each package. In practice, this means there is considerable diversity in the programming languages used as well as the quality of implementation. Quality assurance is community-based; users can and do report bugs, and packages develop reputations for quality and utility. As a result, a limited number of packages tend to get a disproportionate share of usage. Based on data from early 2013,[3] Exhibit 9.3 shows the number of downloads from one widely used CRAN mirror for the top 100 packages.

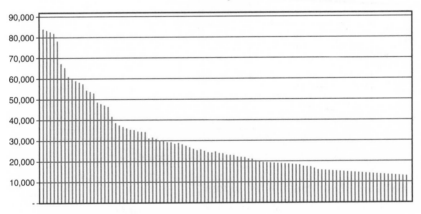

Downloads, Top 100 R Packages
RStudio CRAN Mirror
Jan-May 2013

Exhibit 9.3   R Packages: The Long Tail Effect

[3] Tal Galili, "Top 100 R Packages for 2013 (Jan-May)!" June 13, 2013, http://www.r-statistics.com/2013/06/top-100-r-packages-for-2013-jan-may/.

The R Foundation holds copyright to the R software, which it licenses to users under the GNU General Public License. There are two major commercial distributions of R: Revolution R Enterprise (RRE) and Oracle R Distribution (ORD). TIBCO Software distributes the TIBCO Enterprise Runtime Environment for R (TERR), a commercially licensed variant of R based on the predecessor S-Plus language. Most vendors offering commercial analytics software or data management platforms offer the ability to connect to R programs or embed R scripts in other functions.

The basic R distribution includes a built-in console for interactive use and script development. However, many R users prefer to use integrated development environments (IDEs) or GUI interfaces. The best-known commercial interface for R is RStudio; others include Eclipse, EMACS, R Commander, Rattle, and Revolution Analytics' Revolution Productivity Environment.

R's key strengths are its comprehensive functionality, extensibility, and low cost of ownership. Its key weaknesses are its diverse and bazaar-like approach to development, which produces a plethora of overlapping functionality, loose standards, and heterogeneous software quality. Commercially supported distributions mitigate these weaknesses through quality assurance, training, and support for users.

Another key weakness of R is its inability to handle data sets that exceed the memory of a single machine. There are some open source tools that partially address this problem; in addition, Revolution Analytics' ScaleR package supports distributed out-of-memory analytics for Big Data.

The SAS™ Programming Language

The SAS language is an imperative programming language developed by the SAS Institute, Inc., which also develops tools and software that leverage the SAS programming language. Organizations around the world use SAS; most assessments rank SAS as the industry leader in analytics. Incidence of use for the SAS programming language itself, however, is hard to measure; in broad-based surveys of analysts and data miners, SAS generally ranks well below R and other open source tools.

The SAS programming language consists of two general types of programming steps. SAS DATA steps read data, manipulate the data in various ways, and create SAS DATA sets, a proprietary data structure. SAS PROCs are analytic procedures that operate on SAS DATA sets to produce the particular analysis specified by the user. The results of an SAS PROC may be in the form of a display or report published to a file or an SAS DATA set. The output of one SAS PROC can serve as the input to another SAS PROC.

SAS Institute owns a copyright on its software, which it distributes under license. Most SAS programmers run programs on SAS software; however, other options are available. Courts have ruled that the SAS programming language itself has no copyright protection and is in the public domain. World Programming, Limited, offers a software suite, World Programming System (WPS), which enables users to create, edit, and run programs written in the SAS programming language. DAP, an open source project available under GPL license, provides a scalable runtime environment for SAS programs, albeit with a limited functional scope. Carolina, a commercial software product distributed by Dulles Research, enables users to convert SAS programs to Java; Dulles positions this tool as a migration aid rather than a runtime environment.

SAS offers runtime environments for the SAS programming language for Windows, Linux, Unix, and mainframe operating systems. In addition to these platforms, WPL supports WPS on Mac OS. Most SAS programming steps run single-threaded in the SAS runtime environments; the same programs run multithreaded in WPS.

Responding to some key limitations in the SAS DATA step, SAS has developed DS2, an object-oriented programming language appropriate for advanced data manipulation.[4] SAS DS2 code runs in five environments that do not support the standard SAS DATA step:

- SAS Federated Server
- SAS LASR Analytic Server
- SAS Embedded Process
- SAS Enterprise Miner
- SAS Decision Services

Many SAS programmers work in Display Manager, an IDE bundled with Base SAS. More recently, SAS has offered Enterprise Guide, a Windows-based client application with built-in tools to support code development together with basic reporting capabilities. World Programming offers WPS Workbench, an Eclipse-based IDE for use with the World Programming System.

SQL

SQL, or Structured Query Language, is a language originally designed for use with relational databases. In a recent survey of data scientists conducted by O'Reilly Strata,[5] 71% of respondents reported that they use SQL, more than for any other language (by a wide margin).

Adoption and use of the language, originally developed by IBM researchers in the early 1970s, grew rapidly in the 1980s together with widespread use of relational databases. More recently, use of SQL

---

[4] SAS introduced DS2 after its loss in the *SAS Institute Inc. v World Programming Ltd* court case, in which SAS claimed that the SAS programming language is a domain-specific language and not a general-purpose computer language. Subsequent to the court's decision vacating SAS's claim to own the SAS language, SAS has channeled its development efforts into DS2. As of this writing, SAS's ownership claim to DS2 is uncontested.

[5] O'Reilly Strata, "Data Science Salary Survey: Tools, Trends, What Pays (and What Doesn't) for Data Professionals," January 14, 2014, http://strata.oreilly.com/2014/01/2013-data-science-salary-survey.html.

has expanded beyond conventional relational databases to data warehouse appliances and software-defined SQL platforms (such as Hive or Shark).

SQL is a set-based declarative language rather than an imperative procedural language like SAS or BASIC. The American National Standards Institute (ANSI) defined a SQL standard in 1986, followed closely by the International Organization for Standardization (ISO) in 1987. The SQL standard is well defined, but individual database vendors depart from the standard in various ways that limit the portability of code from one platform to another.

SQL extensions offer procedural programming functionality. The ANSI standard extension is SQL/PSM; vendor-specific extensions include PL/SQL for Oracle, SQL PL for IBM DB2, and SPL for Teradata.

Database administrators use SQL to create and manage databases; with SQL, they can create tables, drop tables, create indexes, insert data into a table, update data in a table, delete data, and perform other operations. Analysts using a relational database as a "sandbox" may also use these SQL capabilities. More typically, analysts use SQL to select and retrieve data from a relational database for use in other analytic operations.

ANSI SQL includes some basic analytics capability, including scalar functions, aggregate functions, and window functions. Scalar functions operate on single values and include such things as numeric operations and string operations. Aggregate functions operate on a collection of values and return a summary value; they include common statistical functions such as count, sum, mean, variance, standard deviation, correlation, and bivariate linear regression. Window functions are similar to aggregate functions but enable the user to apply operations to data partitions, order the data, or define groups of values with moving "windows"; these functions support operations such as cumulative distributions, ranking, and sequencing.

The ANSI SQL standard does not include advanced analytics other than the basic statistics supported as aggregate functions. Database vendors, such as Oracle, offer platform-specific SQL extensions for analytics. More advanced databases that support table functions can embed programs written in general-purpose languages (such as C, Java, Python, or R) and leverage analytic libraries written in these languages.

The key strength of SQL for analytics is its standardization, platform neutrality, and utility for fundamental data manipulation operations. Although vendor-specific versions of SQL depart from the ANSI standard in material ways, most basic operations work in a consistent way across platforms; most users with a strong ANSI SQL background can quickly learn a vendor-specific SQL version. Because SQL platforms are pervasive in large enterprises, a basic understanding of SQL is essential for analysts seeking to retrieve and manipulate data.

The key weakness of SQL for analytics is its lack of standardized algorithms for advanced analytics. Most existing capabilities are vendor-specific extensions or table functions; these are difficult to port across platforms.

Business User Tools

We define a business user interface for analytics as a graphical interface with a workflow metaphor that enables the user to see the project as a series of linked tasks. The market for analytics software with a business user interface is increasingly competitive, with frequent new entrants. We summarize seven leading software products here.

Alteryx

Alteryx, formed in 2010, offers a business user tool (Alteryx Analytics) with data blending and advanced analytics capabilities. Alteryx

Analytics provides analysts with a visual interface that enables users to combine data from many data sources and perform advanced analytics in a single workflow. With Alteryx' data blending tools, users can integrate internal, third party, and cloud-based data; users can perform predictive analytics, spatial analytics, or incorporate custom R code into the workflow. Alteryx users can accomplish these tasks using drag-and-drop tools, with no programming required. Alteryx claims that this approach offers users the ability to save considerable time versus code-based analytics.

Alteryx' key technology partners include Cloudera, Qlik, Revolution Analytics, and Tableau, among others. At present, Alteryx claims more than four hundred customers, including Experian, Kaiser, Ford, and McDonald's, and more than two hundred thousand users.

Alpine

Alpine Data Labs started as an advanced analytics project for database vendor Greenplum; when EMC acquired Greenplum in 2010, Alpine launched as an independent vendor. Originally branded as Alpine Miner, the software is now simply Alpine, and is currently in Release 3.0.

Alpine's analytic features are relatively modest compared to alternatives in the market. A key point of differentiation is Alpine's extension (branded as Alpine Chorus), which serves as a user-friendly catalog for enterprise data.

Platform support for the product is relatively limited, which Alpine masks by leading with its cloud platform. Alpine offers push-down integration with the Pivotal Greenplum database as well as Pivotal, Cloudera, and MapR Hadoop distributions.

IBM SPSS Modeler

Integral Solutions Limited, a U.K.-based software vendor, released this product in 1994 under the brand name Clementine. At the time, ISL claimed that it was the first commercially available analytic software with a graphical user interface. Acquired by SPSS in 1998 and in turn by IBM in 2009, the software features a workflow metaphor widely adopted by analytics vendors seeking to appeal to the business user.

IBM SPSS Modeler supports a wide range of predictive analytics, text analytics, entity analytics, and social network analysis. IBM packages the product in three "editions" (Gold, Professional, and Premium) with progressively richer capabilities. Modeler also supports a custom scripting capability for user-defined analytics.

The Modeler client runs on Windows; server versions run on AIX, Linux, Solaris, and Windows. IBM also supports Modeler in-database operations in a range of databases, including DB2, Oracle, PureData, Sybase, and Teradata. In-database support includes table operations for data preparation, integration with in-database analytic algorithms, and scoring support.

RapidMiner

RapidMiner develops and distributes analytic software (also branded RapidMiner), for which it provides commercial services and support. The company launched in 2006. RapidMiner software started as a predictive analytics project at the Technical University of Dortmund in 2001. The most current version is RapidMiner 6.

RapidMiner software supports a modest range of advanced analytics together with a scripting language for program control. Modeling wizards accelerate the predictive modeling process. The software is highly extensible for custom analytics.

RapidMiner runs natively on Windows and in Java Runtime Environments for Linux, Mac OS, and Unix. Database connectivity is through ODBC; RapidMiner supports pass-through SQL functionality but otherwise does not run inside databases or Hadoop. Scalability is limited to the size of the server on which the software operates.

SAS Enterprise Guide

SAS Enterprise Guide is a Microsoft Windows client application that provides a user-friendly interface to the SAS programming language. SAS positions Enterprise Guide as the primary user interface to SAS and bundles the product with Base SAS at no charge.

SAS insiders estimate that about half of all SAS customers have deployed Enterprise Guide. However, because the software is bundled into Base SAS at no charge, this likely overstates actual usage. Many experienced SAS users simply write code in the Enterprise Guide "code node" and do not rely on the code generation and query generation capabilities, which tend to produce suboptimal code.

SAS Enterprise Miner

SAS Enterprise Miner is SAS's primary platform for machine learning. First introduced in 1998 as a response to Clementine, Quadstone, and other data mining workbenches, the product is now in Release 12.2. Penetration of the product within the SAS customer base is relatively low, at around 10% of all SAS customers.

Enterprise Miner offers a comprehensive set of machine learning algorithms,[6] including popular favorites such as decision trees, neural networks, and support vector machines.

Enterprise Miner is a data-mining workbench with a visual interface based on a workflow metaphor. The look and feel of the interface is similar to Enterprise Guide and other SAS end-user products.

SAS Enterprise Miner uses distributed environments through SAS Grid Manager and high-performance appliances through SAS High-Performance Analytics Server. The most common deployment, however, is on a single server; in this case, Enterprise Miner suffers

---

[6] See http://www.sas.com/technologies/analytics/datamining/miner/index.html#section=3.

from the same issues as Legacy SAS. SAS Enterprise Miner leverages data sources through SAS/ACCESS, as described under Legacy SAS. Unlike Legacy SAS, Enterprise Miner can export predictive models to PMML, C, or Java. Enterprise Miner can also export scoring functions through SAS Scoring Accelerator.

Statistica

Statistica is a suite of software for advanced analytics distributed by StatSoft, a firm located in Tulsa, Oklahoma. (In March 2014, Dell announced that it acquired StatSoft.) Originally developed in 1984, the most current version of the product is Statistica 12.0.

The Statistica suite includes 14 modules that support statistics, multivariate analysis, data mining, ETL, real-time scoring, quality control, process control, and vertical solutions. Relative to other software products on the market, functionality is comprehensive.

StatSoft supports client and server editions of Statistica on Windows only. StatSoft is able to exploit multiple processors on a single machine but does not support distributed processing, in-database, or in-Hadoop operations. Statistica ETL supports connectors to Oracle and SQL Server. Statistica's analytic modules export PMML for remote scoring.

Summary

In this chapter, we summarized the typical user personas in the modern enterprise. Sophisticated users, including power analysts and data scientists, tend to use analytic languages such as R, SAS, or SQL. Business users, including business analysts and analytic consumers, tend to use business-friendly software; we reviewed six of the many available software products in this category. Exhibit 9.4 shows the tools appropriate for each user persona.

Exhibit 9.4 Typical Tools Used by Analytic Personas

	Programming Languages	Business User Tools
Power Analyst	**R** **SAS**	**SAS Display Manager** **SAS Enterprise Guide**
Data Scientist	Java MapReduce Python **R** Scala	n/a
Business Analyst	N/A	**Alpine** **IBM SPSS Modeler** **Rapid Minder** **SAS Enterprise Guide** **SAS Enterprise Miner** **Statistica**
Analytics Consumer	N/A	MS-Excel Web BI Tools Business Applications

Bold denotes tools with detailed descriptions in this chapter.

Enterprises should support the needs of all user personas and do so in a manner that supports collaboration and customization. Users with different personas do not work in isolation; sophisticated users should be able to share applications with business users and vice versa.

Data complexity and opaqueness tend to drive users toward programming tools; a clean and transparent data architecture is an essential enabler for business-friendly analytics.

10

Analytic Platforms

Overview

What is the best platform for analytics? Many competing options are available to organizations today: traditional server-based software, in-database analytics, in-memory analytics, cloud-based analytics, and so forth. In the previous chapter, we reviewed various tools that enable end users to interact with the analytic computing environment. In this chapter, we focus on the analytic computing itself, as shown in Exhibit 10.1.

Data is the raw material for analytics, and analytics defines value for data; it follows that the most important dimension for any analytic architecture is the means by which the computing engine integrates with data. Integration with data sources affects the scope of tasks performed by analysts, the training they need, and the cycle time for an analysis project.

In this chapter, we review generic architectures for advanced analytics, in two parts. In the first part, we review generic architectures for predictive analytics; in the second, we discuss high-performance SQL platforms.

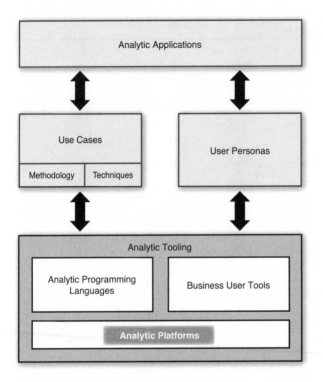

Exhibit 10.1   Modern Analytics Framework

Predictive Analytics Architecture

In Chapter 8, "Predictive Analytics Methodology," we reviewed the complex sequence of tasks in the predictive analytics workflow. Although the exact sequence of tasks depends on the problem and may differ across organizations, the diagram shown in Exhibit 10.2 is typical.

When you consider practical options to integrate analytics and data, four distinct architectures emerge:

- **Freestanding analytics**—All analytic tasks run on a platform that is independent of all data source platforms.

- **Partially integrated analytics**—Model development tasks run on an independent platform, but data preparation and model deployment tasks run in data sources.

- **In-Database analytics**—All analytic tasks run inside a massively parallel database.

- **In-Hadoop analytics**—All analytic tasks run inside Hadoop.

We discuss each of these options in the sections that follow.

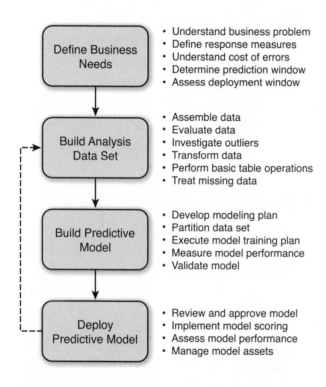

Exhibit 10.2   Predictive Analytics Methodology

Freestanding Analytics

In the freestanding analytics architecture (see Exhibit 10.3), analysts perform all required tasks on a workstation or server that is independent of all data sources. Users extract raw data from sources in atomic form and then aggregate and cleanse the data in the analysis environment. After preparing the data, the user performs advanced analysis and retains predictive models within the analysis environment. To apply the models, users extract production data again, score it natively within the analytics engine, and return the model scores to the production environment for upload and use.

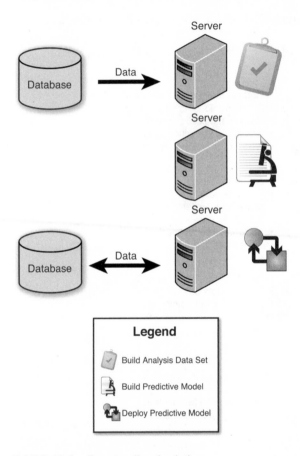

Exhibit 10.3 Freestanding Analytics

This architecture was the only method available for many years, and is still standard practice in a surprisingly large number of organizations. Scoring in a freestanding analytics environment is labor intensive and makes high demands on the analytics team's time; as a result, this architecture is not well suited to any application requiring fresh, low-latency model scores. Consequently, most organizations with significant investment in analytics have moved away from this architecture or are actively considering doing so.

In some situations, this architecture works reasonably well. They include applications requiring only small snippets of data, applications whose product is insight in the form of a report or graph rather than a predictive model, and "one-off" projects that do not warrant a production implementation. Research applications, such as simulation or complex analysis of variance, often fall into this category and derive greater benefit from memory-based platforms (such as GPU "sidecars" or in-memory databases than from data integration *per se*).

Partially Integrated Analytics

In a partially integrated architecture (see Exhibit 10.4), users perform some tasks in the source data platform and others in a freestanding analytics platform. Typically, users perform data processing tasks inside the data source and push scoring to a target database or decision engine. This approach aligns tasks and tools to maximize productivity.

For data source integration, instead of extracting all data at an atomic level and building the analytic data set "bottoms-up" in the analytic environment, the analyst uses native tooling (for example, SQL and/or ETL tools) in the data source to build the analysis data set. The analyst then extracts and moves the finished data set to the analytics environment to complete the data preparation tasks (using techniques not available in the database environment) and to perform model-building operations.

Although analysts can perform these operations directly in native tools, many prefer interfaces provided by a preferred analytics vendor. There are two distinctly different types of data source interfaces: "Pass Through" and "Push Down." SAS, for example, offers "Pass Through" integration enabling the analyst to embed SQL, HiveQL, Pig, or MapReduce commands in an SAS program—SAS controls the overall flow of execution and logs in to the target data source as a remote user to run the commands. This approach is highly flexible, but the user must explicitly specify the appropriate syntax to use, and it requires a strong understanding of the relevant programming language.

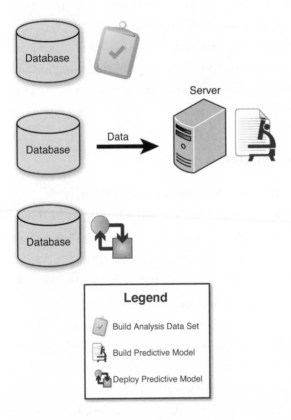

Exhibit 10.4   Partially Integrated Analytics

IBM SPSS, Alpine, and other vendors offer "Push Down" integration that *translates* user requests into platform-specific commands. "Push Down" integration is much easier to use because the analyst needs no special knowledge of programming languages. It tends to be inherently less flexible because the interface itself supports a finite use case.

For scoring and prediction, instead of scoring new data in the analytics environment, the analyst produces an object or executable code and passes it to the production database for in-database scoring. Most analytic software packages export models into popular programming languages (such as C, Java, or Python) or Predictive Model Markup Language (PMML), but there are some important exceptions; for example, "Legacy" SAS software (Base SAS, SAS/STAT, and so on) exports models exclusively in a proprietary SAS format. SAS Enterprise Miner exports models as C, Java, or PMML, with some limitations. SAS Scoring Accelerator exports proprietary scoring functions to selected databases, but it works only with SAS Enterprise Miner.

Unfortunately, automated scoring model integration works only if the schema of the analytical model-building environment aligns with the schema of the target environment for the scoring model. The analytic schema does not have to be an exact copy of the production schema; it can be a subset but cannot be a superset. Field naming and other conventions must align; otherwise, the production database or decision engine will not be able to interpret the scoring model produced by the analytics application.

When it is not possible to align the schemas of the analytic and production environments, the only recourse is manual scoring model development, a task that can add up to six months to the project life cycle. Manual programming is still the norm in a surprisingly large number of organizations.

In-Database Analytics

We use the term *in-database analytics* to refer to an architecture where the predictive analytics engine runs on the same physical platform with a database (see Exhibit 10.5). All tasks run in the same physical environment, and data does not move from one platform to another.

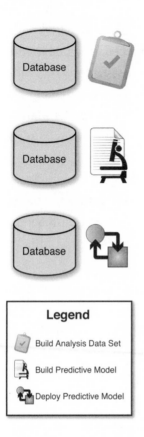

Exhibit 10.5 In-Database Analytics

Leading relational databases such as DB2 and Oracle and MPP databases such as IBM PureData and Teradata all include advanced analytics capabilities. In-database analytics tooling is not new: Teradata first introduced Warehouse Miner in 1987; in 1993, IBM introduced DB2 Intelligent Miner. Oracle acquired the data mining software assets of Thinking Machines in 1999 and integrated the software with Oracle Database beginning in 2003.

More recently, the emergence, adoption, and growth of MPP databases such as IBM PureData for Analytics (Netezza) and Pivotal Database (Greenplum) have sparked renewed interest in merging analytic engines with the database engine. IBM PureData offers a library of distributed machine learning algorithms called IBM Netezza

Analytics. Oracle offers a similar library called the Oracle Advanced Analytics Option. Pivotal Database lacks native analytics, but the vendor works with customers to use the MADLib open source library for machine learning. Teradata takes a vendor-neutral stance toward analytics and supports in-database offerings from Fuzzy Logix, Revolution Analytics, SAS, and TIBCO, among others.

In the absence of cross-platform standards for in-database analytics, each vendor has developed its own unique libraries; database vendors use analytics to differentiate their product in the marketplace. Unfortunately, this lack of standards inhibits adoption. Many organizations have a multi-vendor data architecture, and users cannot simply transfer models from one platform to another.

There are two general approaches to cross-platform in-database analytics. One approach is to build an analytics library and support it in multiple platforms through table functions. An independent analytics vendor, Fuzzy Logix, uses this approach to offer its DB Lytix library on multiple database platforms. As of this writing, DB Lytix is available on IBM Informix, IBM PureData, Microsoft SQL Server, Par Accel, SAP Sybase, Teradata Database, and Teradata Aster.

In another approach to cross-platform standards, several MPP database vendors encourage the use of open source R. This approach works for embarrassingly parallel or data parallel applications, but integration can be challenging and vendor support tends to be limited. HP Vertica promotes the use of its distributed computing framework (Presto) with open source R on the Vertica platform. IBM PureData distributes several R packages enabling R users to submit work from the R console.

Oracle has its own R distributions: Oracle R Distribution and Oracle R Enterprise. They include features for pushing R functions into Oracle Database and the Oracle Big Data Appliance. Teradata works with Revolution Analytics to support Revolution R Enterprise in Teradata Database.

Certain use cases are well suited to an in-database architecture, including predictive model scoring, analytics on large data sets where it is important to use all of the data, and analytics with curated data that cannot leave the repository. The latter case is typical for clinical trial data, for one example, but organizations seeking to enforce data security often impose physical controls over data movement. An in-database analytics architecture is essential for these organizations.

Analytics in Hadoop

Although the benefits of in-Hadoop analytics are similar to the benefits of in-database analytics, we distinguish between the two because the technical options for advanced analytics in Hadoop are completely different. Hadoop is still at an early stage of development; query tools for Hadoop are less mature than in MPP databases, and Hadoop is generally much more difficult to work with than an MPP database.

Hadoop is particularly well suited to serve as an analytics platform due to its significantly lower cost compared to MPP databases and because the Hadoop file system supports diverse data without pre-structuring. For this reason, options for advanced analytics in Hadoop are expanding rapidly.

Until recently, options for advanced analytics in Hadoop were very limited; available open source projects were rudimentary, and required high levels of user skill. For the most part, analysts had to write their own algorithms in MapReduce or another programming language.

By design, MapReduce makes a single pass through data and then persists the result set; this approach works reasonably well for embarrassingly parallel and data parallel problems, but it impedes performance for graph-parallel, iterative, and streaming analytics. In the first chapter of Hadoop's history (Hadoop 1.0), analytic developers built on MapReduce because it was the only way to integrate analytics into a mixed workload. The most important open source projects for analytics from this era are Apache Hive, Apache Mahout, and Apache Giraph.

Apache Hive provides users with tools for summarization, query, and analysis using a variation of SQL called HiveQL. Developers at Facebook started working on Hive in 2007 and released an open source version in 2008. We cover Hive in a later section on SQL in Hadoop.

The Apache Mahout project, started in 2008, supports a library of machine learning algorithms designed for use with Hadoop. Although most Hadoop distributions include Mahout, the project has never attracted a significant community of users or developers, and it has no significant commercial backing. Mahout is rich in unsupervised learning capabilities, but many of its algorithms remain partially developed with no significant support. The project team plans to deprecate weakly supported algorithms prior to 1.0 status.

Apache Giraph is a highly scalable graph engine based on Google's Pregel graph engine project. Giraph launched as an Apache incubator project in 2012. Facebook reports that it uses Giraph to support a social graph with more than a trillion edges. Giraph, like Mahout, interfaces with the Hadoop Distributed File System (HDFS) and runs natively within MapReduce.

In addition to the open source projects cited previously, three commercially licensed software products integrate with Hadoop through MapReduce. They include Alpine Data Labs' Alpine software; IBM SPSS Analytic Server, a back-end component that translates user requests from IBM SPSS Modeler into MapReduce commands; and Revolution Analytics' ScaleR package, which converts an R user's requests to MapReduce.

With the development of YARN for workload management, developers are now able to introduce analytics that leverage the Hadoop file systems but bypass MapReduce. The most significant open source projects to emerge in this new chapter are Impala, Shark, and Stinger for fast queries; H2O and Spark MLLib for machine learning; GraphLab and Spark GraphX for graph engines; and Spark Streaming for streaming analytics. (We discuss the fast query projects in the "SQL-on-Hadoop" section later in this chapter.)

H2O is an open source project supported by startup 0xdata ("Hexadata"). The project includes a library of distributed in-memory algorithms and runs either on a freestanding cluster or in Hadoop. 0xdata offers its software to the community at no charge and then negotiates agreements for services and support.

Apache Spark is a platform for in-memory computing within Hadoop. Spark supports several subprojects, including MLLib for machine learning, GraphX for graph engines, Shark for fast queries, and Spark Streaming for streaming analytics. Spark works with all Hadoop file formats and supports interfaces with Scala, Java, Python, and R. As of February 2014, Cloudera includes Spark in its Hadoop distribution, with commercial support provided by startup Databricks.

GraphLab is a graph-based distributed computing framework. Developed at Carnegie Mellon University in 2009, the project is now in Release 2.2 and has attracted a large community of developers and users. GraphLab includes a number of libraries (toolkits) supporting graph analytics (for example, PageRank and triangle counting); graphical models; topic modeling (including document clustering and topical representations); clustering; collaborative filtering; and tools for reasoning about images. GraphLab, Inc., a startup launched in 2013, offers commercial support for the GraphLab open source project.

Commercial software vendors offer two additional options for advanced analytics in Hadoop. Analytics leader SAS offers its in-memory High Performance Analytics software; this is essentially the same software offered by SAS for implementation in appliances. Startup Skytree offers distributed machine learning software (Skytree Server) originally developed at Georgia Tech's FastLab. As of this writing, customer acceptance of these products appears to be limited, but further development and adoption of YARN may make these products more attractive.

Analytics in the Cloud

Organizations can implement any of the previous architectures on premises or "in the cloud." A detailed discussion of the various types of cloud computing is outside the scope of this book; in this section, we briefly discuss the role cloud computing can play in an overall analytics architecture.

Cloud computing is distributed computing with pooled resources. The end user exercises limited control over the physical hardware used to provide workload—that is, the user submits jobs to the cloud. Computing clouds may be public clouds (such as Amazon Web Services) or private clouds dedicated to an enterprise. Public cloud services can consist simply of IT infrastructure leased for a definite period, or they can consist of specific applications (such as those provided on the Amazon Marketplace). Private clouds may include the enterprise's own computing hardware, shared resources, or a mix.

Startups and smaller analytic service providers generally rely on a public cloud. In larger organizations, a private cloud may be an option as well; firms with unique security and privacy requirements tend to prefer private cloud to public cloud computing.

There are five distinct situations favoring cloud-based analytics.

- Firms with limited funds to invest in IT infrastructure
- Analytic service providers who bill costs to clients
- Analytic teams with highly variable and unpredictable workloads
- Enterprises with predictable peak workloads
- Analytic teams with weak IT support

Startup ventures frequently lack available capital to purchase IT infrastructure. While cloud-based infrastructure may be more expensive on an average cost basis, economies of scale in the cloud enable small, growing firms to grow quickly. The convenience and flexibility of cloud-based architecture permits the firm to focus on its core mission.

Analytic service providers include consultants, advertising agencies, analytic "boutiques," and similar firms. These firms may also be startups, so the points covered in the previous paragraph about conserving capital may also apply. Service providers have the additional problem that it is often very difficult for them to forecast workload— adding a single client could double the analytic workload. These firms also bill expenses back to clients and must attribute every unit of work to a specific client account. Cloud computing platforms simplify this accounting and billing problem.

Advanced analytics is computationally intensive; it tends to produce "lumpy" and unpredictable workloads. (This is why database administrators are often reluctant to permit analytic users to develop models in the database). If the organization provides dedicated infrastructure to the analytics team to support its peak workload, that computing resource will sit idle most of the time. Thus, it makes good sense to support the analytics team with either private or public cloud infrastructure.

Analytic applications can also produce workloads that are highly variable but very predictable. Banks, for example, run Basel reports monthly; query and report workloads spike at the end of the month as managers compare performance to plan; analytic workloads for retailers shift heavily from planning in the spring to reporting in the Christmas season. Once again, it makes good sense for the organization to distinguish between base workload and peak workload and to support peak workload with cloud computing.

Finally, cloud platforms make good sense for analytic teams with poor internal IT support. Analysts in business units seeking to move quickly may conflict with their IT support team, especially in conservative organizations motivated by cost control or procedural concerns.

Marketing, in particular, tends to operate on a rapid cadence. In this situation, the analytics team may find that public cloud computing enables them to respond more quickly to the needs of their internal clients.

Two principle concerns limit adoption of cloud computing for analytics: security and data movement. Security concerns are more a matter of perceptions than reality—on-premises systems can be hacked—but perceptions do matter. This issue affects public clouds more than private clouds.

The need to upload data can also limit use of cloud for analysis of very large data sets; the time and effort needed to move the data may be unacceptable. This is not an issue, of course, when the source data for the analysis is already in the cloud (as is the case for some organizations). The other point to keep in mind is that data movement may be necessary whether the analysis runs on premises or in the cloud; when this is the case, moving data to the cloud takes no more time than moving it from one system to another on premises.

The logic of workload management suggests that predictive model development will increasingly move to the cloud, as analysts adopt more computationally intensive techniques. Model scoring, which is embarrassingly parallel and I/O intensive, will follow the data; organizations will keep this task close to the data, on-premises or in the cloud as the case may be.

Modern SQL Platforms

SQL, or Structured Query Language, was developed in the early 1970s at IBM. By the early 1980s, SQL became the de facto database language largely in thanks to Oracle promoting it as such. During this period, databases were primarily designed to create and modify individual transactions and became known as online transaction processing (OLTP). These workloads were optimized for individual records and, as such, were used to capture transaction data but were not typically used for analytic workloads, which tend to process data in aggregates or by columns. Over the last few decades, the SQL standard has been extended to include basic calculations as functions in the language. Examples of basic functions include average, minimum, maximum, and count.

The popularization of data warehouses in the early 1980s to store large quantities of data presented the opportunity to start analyzing the data. In the mid-1990s, in-database analytics were initially introduced, and that started the convergence of SQL based databases with analytics. In-database analytics provided database users the opportunity to embed more complex analytics into the database where the computation could occur without extracting the data from the data warehouse. However, writing complex analytics code is challenging and it wasn't until the mid-2000s that in-database analytics started gaining popularity. To make it easier for database users, vendors started embedding rich analytic libraries into database platforms. While there are benefits to in-database analytics, the technology still remains underutilized in the marketplace.

What Is a Modern SQL Platform?

Edgar Codd initially introduced SQL as a database language to make it easier for people to create and manipulate relational database tables. Within a decade, SQL was the de facto language for databases, and today it is the most powerful, mature, and widely accepted language for databases. Although SQL platforms usually have an interactive capability with which a user can pose a query and get results, many of the production processing is executed offline in batch processing.

Traditional, general-purpose databases are categorized as OLTP databases. OLTP databases have been around since the 1970s and are quite mature. As OLTP databases matured, database vendors converged on relational (row-based) databases that provided varying capabilities to guarantee reliable processing of transactions in the database. Today this set of data integrity properties collectively is referred to as ACID (Atomic, Consistent, Isolation, Durability) compliance.

Traditionally, a data warehouse is a specialized relational database designed for reporting and online analytical processing (OLAP). Data warehouses are also quite mature and conform to ACID.

The traditional database and data warehouse market was disrupted in 2006 with the introduction of Hadoop, an open source software framework for the distributed storage and processing of large unstructured data on commodity hardware. Hadoop was designed to be resilient and fault tolerant[1] across clusters of machines.

Hadoop created an opening for new innovation in the database market that is still unfolding today. Around 2009, NoSQL databases emerged, which differed from traditional databases in the following ways:

- Nonrelational, distributed data stores
- No SQL capability
- Non-ACID compliant

NoSQL databases have used various data store architectures, including tree, graph, and key-value pairs. As NoSQL databases have matured, they've introduced an "eventually consistent" data integrity model that eventually provides ACID-compliant data integrity.

Although initially the NoSQL databases didn't include a SQL capability, as the NoSQL databases have evolved, they typically have a SQL-like capability, and the NoSQL came to represent "Not Only SQL." One of the most important contributions of this technology is that these databases broke through the horizontal scaling barrier typical in traditional OLTP and data warehouses. Horizontal scaling

---

[1] Fault tolerance is feature that enables the system to gracefully handle unexpected software and hardware interruptions such as power outages, disabled networks, and more.

indicates the ability to add computing nodes beyond the physical machine without any limitations in the database processing. This important breakthrough allowed NoSQL databases to take advantage of commodity hardware, thus driving down the cost of database and data warehousing applications significantly. Fault tolerance is another important capability of NoSQL databases.

In 2011, fast on the heels of the introduction of NoSQL databases, the industry introduced NewSQL platforms that borrowed capabilities from traditional databases, data warehouses, and NoSQL databases. Fundamentally, NewSQL platforms provide horizontal scaling, faster transaction processing, fault tolerance, SQL interface, and ACID compliance.

A modern SQL platform differs from legacy SQL platforms in a few important ways, providing

- Horizontal scale out on commodity hardware
- Ability to easily ingest and process any data
- Higher performance querying and analytics processing throughput
- Data integrity and consistency
- A user configurable balance between distributed processing and fault tolerance

A modern SQL platform uses a distributed processing architecture on commodity hardware to deliver virtually limitless horizontal scale-out with fault tolerance. Although modern SQL platforms provide ACID compliance and higher processing throughput, there is no free lunch. To be able to deliver consistency, these platforms need to lock data to make changes. Each platform either by default makes the trade-off between performance and consistency or allows the user to make that trade-off.

A modern SQL platform goes beyond support for large character and string data to fully manage unlimited, variable-length characters.

Furthermore, modern SQL platforms provide fast processing on huge data sets—web scale data sets—not just limited subsets of the data.

Today, there are three primary modern SQL platforms:

1. MPP (massively parallel processing) databases
2. SQL-on-Hadoop
3. NewSQL databases

Each modern SQL platform supports one or more styles of analytical querying and processing, including

- **Batch SQL**—Behind-the-scenes execution of queries on data-at-rest that takes time to process. High latency querying with typical run times ranging from 20 minutes to 20 hours. This style is commonly used for large ETL processing, data mining, and predictive model building.

- **Interactive SQL**—Online execution of queries on data-at-rest that executes while the user is awaiting a response. Lower latency queries with typical run times ranging from 100 milliseconds to 20 minutes. This style is commonly used for traditional business intelligence reporting and visualizations, ad hoc querying, and reporting.

- **Real-time or Operational SQL**—High-concurrency transactional processing of queries on data-at-rest by large numbers of users. Low latency queries with typical run time under 100 milliseconds. This style is commonly used for read-only operations on large data (OLAP), point queries, and web applications for smaller data sets.

- **Streaming SQL**—Continuous query and analytic processing of data-in-motion in real-time typically over a sliding window of time (for example, "How many anomalies have been detected in the last 5 minutes?"). Very low latency queries with typical run time under 10 milliseconds. This style is commonly used for algorithmic trading, real-time ad targeting, real-time fraud detection, and real-time network intrusion.

SQL supports analytics through several mechanisms:

- **SQL built-in functions**—Basic descriptive analytic functions implemented in SQL, such as average, count, percentile, standard deviation, and others.
- **SQL user-defined functions (UDFs)**—They provide a mechanism for users to write their own analytic functions typically in a lower-level programming language such as Java, C, or C++.
- **SQL analytic libraries**—Analytic functions implemented in SQL and SQL user-defined functions. These are typically third-party libraries and can include statistics, predictive analytics, machine learning, and others. DB Lytix from Fuzzy Logix and open source MadLib are examples of such libraries.

The following sections provide further descriptions of modern SQL platforms with key differences from the norm highlighted.

MPP Databases

A massively parallel processing (MPP) database typically uses a shared nothing architecture that distributes the data and workload from a single server to many independent computing nodes. Dividing and conquering the workload increases the processing throughput of database operations. In traditional databases, computations are computed centrally by marshaling all the data onto the central node and then performing the computation. With MPP databases, data movement bottlenecks are avoided by moving the query and computation to the data.

MPP databases are the most commercially adopted data warehouses currently.

Appliance Concept

An appliance is a combination of hardware and software that is optimized for the hardware. Data warehouse appliances, typically include an MPP database along with the hardware to support the MPP database, are the most mature appliances in the market today. An appliance goes beyond mere "packaging" of the hardware and software to a purpose-built database appliance that tightly integrates and tunes both the hardware and software.

Pros and Cons

Pros	Cons
Vertical scaling (handle large volume of rows)	Little or no horizontal scaling (adding of additional nodes or servers to handle new/increasing workloads)
Batch and interactive SQL capable	Little or no support for real-time or streaming SQL
ACID compliance	Specialized, premium-priced hardware
Strong enterprise operational features	

Commercial Products

There are several commercial MPP products available. While this is not a full list of MPP vendors, these products are typical considerations for enterprises and are included here as they illustrate key differences in approaches.

HP Vertica

HP Vertica is a columnar store MPP data warehouse designed for analytical processing via batch and interactive SQL workloads. With its columnar store capability, HP Vertica has a strong environment for historical analysis and especially time series analysis. It has a row capability that overlays the columnar store, but performance suffers significantly. HP Vertica capabilities include in-database analytics and high-speed connectors to other data sources, including files, databases, and Hadoop. Additionally, HP Vertica includes useful analytical SQL functions and support for R.

IBM PureData (Formerly Known as Netezza)

The IBM PureData family of appliances are preconfigured MPP appliances that are purpose built for performance-demanding data warehousing and analytic workloads that support both batch and interactive SQL processing. The IBM PureData appliances are well known for using a field programmable gate array (FPGA) to offload SQL preprocessing from the CPU to speed up query and analytic execution.

IBM PureData is also an established market leader in data warehousing that initially disrupted the market through the use of FPGAs and by simplifying the data warehouse setup and ongoing administration of the data warehouse. IBM PureData capabilities include in-database analytics and high-speed connectors to other data sources including files, databases, and Hadoop. In addition to the out-of-box analytics and support for R in PureData, customers can purchase a variety of analytic software add-ons, most notably IBM SPSS Modeler.

Oracle Exadata

The Oracle Exadata family of MPP appliances are designed for first generation/traditional OLTP and OLAP/Business Intelligence requirements that support both batch and interactive SQL processing.

Exadata provides analytics through a variety of software add-ons, including Oracle R Enterprise, Oracle Data Mining, Oracle Advanced Analytics Option, and a connector to Hadoop.

Pivotal Greenplum Database

Pivotal Greenplum Database is MPP database software designed for data warehousing and analytics workloads through batch and interactive SQL workloads. Pivotal offers appliances through partnerships with hardware vendors.

Teradata

The Teradata family of appliances are highly configurable, enterprise-tested, data warehouse appliances that support both batch and interactive SQL processing.

Teradata is an established market leader in data warehousing and has a wide variety of capabilities that support analytics processing, including in-database analytics and high-speed connectors to other data sources including files, databases, and Hadoop. Teradata provides analytics through a variety of software add-ons.

SQL-on-Hadoop

SQL-on-Hadoop is defined as a SQL engine that co-exists with data on Hadoop nodes. The SQL engine processes batch and interactive SQL queries directly against Hadoop data sources.

Note that SQL-on-Hadoop is not the same as a Hadoop connector. Connectors transfer data back and forth between the databases that are connected to Hadoop. Although some of the connectors are parallelized to increase throughput, the data movement, especially on large volumes, makes it an untenable solution for anything other than the convenience of occasional ad hoc querying.

Pros and Cons

Pros	Cons
Ability to query large volumes of mixed data types	Little or no support for real-time or streaming SQL
Batch and interactive SQL capable	Lacking in operational support feature
Schema-less data environment	
Fault tolerant	

Commercial Products

There are several open source and commercial SQL-on-Hadoop products available. While this is not a full list of SQL-on-Hadoop products, these are typical considerations for enterprises and are included here as they illustrate key differences in approaches.

Apache Hive

Apache Hive is an open source data warehouse infrastructure with a query language called Hive Query Language (HQL) that implements queries as Map Reduce jobs. Hive queries are batch queries that can be executed against multiple data stores, including HDFS and MySQL databases.

Cloudera Impala

Cloudera's Impala is an MPP database engine that resides on each Hadoop node for executing batch and interactive SQL queries. Typically, Impala uses MapReduce to perform data processing against the same data to eliminate data movement. Impala does support basic UDFs in addition to open source analytic packages.

Hortonworks Stinger

Stinger is an open source project sponsored by Hortonworks to improve data warehouse processing on Hadoop. The project includes significant improvements to data processing as well as query processing with a goal of adding interactive SQL processing to the existing batch SQL querying. Stinger includes the ability to implement in-database analytics via Java-based UDFs.

Hadapt

Hadapt provides SQL query engines that run on Hadoop nodes. One engine is designed for long-running batch SQL queries and is implemented via MapReduce. The interactive SQL queries are implemented via PostgresSQL (an open source database engine). Hadapt includes the ability to implement in-database analytics via Java-based UDFs.

Teradata SQL-H

A Teradata database and Hadoop connector allow data in Hadoop to be accessible via the Teradata SQL query engine by using the Hadoop metadata (via HCatalog) to seamlessly plan batch queries across the Teradata and Hadoop data stores.

Splice Machine

Splice Machine is a parallelized SQL engine based on Apache Derby (an open source Java-based database) that replaces Derby tables with HBase data files to provide interactive SQL queries. Splice Machine runs on top of standard Hadoop distributions, including Cloudera, Hortonworks, and MapR.

NewSQL Databases

NewSQL databases are the next generation of SQL transactional (OLTP) databases. The key distinction of NewSQL databases is a SQL-based, ACID-compliant distributed architecture with unlimited horizontal scale-out. NewSQL databases deliver a wider range of SQL capabilities including batch, interactive, real-time, and in some cases, streaming.

Pros and Cons

Pros	Cons
Blend OLTP and OLAP into one high-performance database	None are fully featured yet
Horizontal scaling on commodity hardware	Most do not yet have in-database or out-of-box analytic capabilities
ANSI standard SQL	
Ability to query and process large volumes of mixed data types	
Real-time performance	
ACID compliance	
Fault tolerant	
Typically have strong API/connectors	
A few have real-time and streaming analytic support	

Commercial Products

There are several commercial NewSQL products available. While this is not a full list of NewSQL vendors, these are typical considerations for enterprises and are included here as they illustrate key differences in approaches.

Clustrix

Clustrix is a high-performance, in-memory, distributed, ACID-compliant, fault-tolerant, relational database with the full range of SQL queries: batch, interactive, real-time, and streaming. Clustrix can be deployed on-premise, virtualized, or in the cloud (public or private).

Google Spanner

Google Spanner is a fault-tolerant, globally distributed, open source, semi-relational database that supports SQL queries: batch and interactive. This internally built and used database is available via open source. It is not generally designed for analytics.

MemSQL

MemSQL is an extremely high-performance, distributed in-memory and columnar, commodity-based, ACID-compliant, fault-tolerant relational database with the full range of SQL queries: batch, interactive, real-time, and streaming. MemSQL can be deployed on-premise, virtualized, or in the cloud (public or private). MemSQL uniquely converts SQL into C++ using a just-in-time compiler to get extremely high-performance SQL execution. The blazing fast performance often eliminates traditional batch-oriented ETL processing because the ingest rate is fast enough to perform transformations as the data is being ingested.

NuoDB

NuoDB is a globally distributed, cloud-based, multitenant, ACID-compliant, fault-tolerant relational database with support for a range of SQL queries: batch, interactive, and real-time.

Pivotal SQLFire

Pivotal SQLFire is an in-memory, distributed, ACID-compliant, fault-tolerant relational database with a range of SQL queries: batch, interactive, and real-time. Pivotal SQLFire can be deployed on-premise or in the cloud (public or private).

SAP HANA

SAP HANA is an in-memory, columnar store, ACID-compliant, fault-tolerant database with batch and interactive SQL queries. SAP HANA is optimized and available only on certified hardware platforms (currently HP, Fujitsu, Cisco, IBM, Hitachi, Lenovo, and Dell).

In addition to a SQL interface, HANA provides an MDX (query language for OLAP/Business Intelligence applications). HANA is offered on-premise or via the cloud.

TransLattice

TransLattice is a globally distributed, ACID-compliant, fault-tolerant relational database that supports SQL queries: batch and interactive. TransLattice can be deployed on-premise, virtualized, or in the cloud (public or private). Although TransLattice is a NewSQL database, it is not designed for analytics.

VoltDB

VoltDB is a high-performance, in-memory and columnar, distributed, ACID-compliant, fault-tolerant relational database with the full range of SQL queries: batch, interactive, real-time, and streaming. VoltDB can be deployed on-premise, virtualized, or in the cloud (public or private).

Where Is the Future for Modern SQL Platforms?

Modern SQL platforms are disrupting the legacy database market. The trend started slowly with the introduction of MPP databases in the early 1980s and has quickly moved into the fast lane with the introduction of Hadoop in 2006. Since then, there has been a quick succession of significantly improved database architectures starting with NoSQL, then SQL-on-Hadoop, and now with NewSQL platforms.

MPP databases are quickly becoming legacy environments but exist in many data centers. Fast-moving technology upstarts, primarily in new industries in digital media and gaming, have often bypassed the MPP platforms in favor of newer platforms such as Hadoop, NoSQL, or NewSQL environments. Make no mistake about it, though; MPP databases will be around for quite some time because they are well entrenched in the data centers of many industries: financial services, telecommunications, retailers, health care, and many others. SQL-on-Hadoop gives customers trying to derive value from their Hadoop data lakes an opportunity to derive value from their big data. However, the current constraints of Hadoop in processing large mixed-data analytic workloads in real-time with the enterprise readiness that many industries require is limiting. The NewSQL platforms, while still not as mature as either MPP or SQL-on-Hadoop platforms, are demonstrating the ability to drive real-time scalability on mixed data and analytic workloads.

There is also a new landscape emerging, coined Hybrid Transaction and Analytical Processing (HTAP) by Gartner. This landscape is predicated on in-memory processing databases (IMDBMS) to provide real-time analytics processing while simultaneously ingesting web scale data. Databases that support HTAP significantly simplify the infrastructure by eliminating the need for separate transaction and analytic databases. While this concept has been around for decades, the underlying technology is finally mature enough to support the strenuous workload demands. This provides businesses with opportunities to innovate new real-time analytic applications that don't simply speed up existing analytic applications, but instead allow businesses to embed analytics into operational processes and create better, immediate situational awareness.

Exhibit 10.6 illustrates the strengths and weaknesses of the three major modern SQL platforms.

	MPP	SQL-on-Hadoop	NewSQL
Primary Data Storage	Relational	File Based	Relational
Distributed	●	◕	●
Horizontal Scale-out	◔	◕	●
Data at Rest	●	●	●
Data in Motion	◐	○	●
Unstructured Data	◔	◐	◐
OLTP Processing	○	○	●
OLAP Processing	●	●	◐

Exhibit 10.6   Modern SQL Platforms Summary

Summary

In this chapter, we reviewed analytic architecture in two parts. In the first part, we covered platforms for predictive analytics, including freestanding server-based analytics, partially integrated analytics, in-database analytics, and analytics in Hadoop. In the second part, we covered high-performance SQL platforms. Next, we'll turn our attention to the people side of the equation—the talent required to deliver analytic solutions for your organization.

Section III

Implement Your Analytics Roadmap

11

Attracting and Retaining Analytics Talent

Overview

The analytics roadmap is the first stepping-stone in turning a business strategy into analytics execution to achieve your business goals. Implementing or deploying your analytics is where the proverbial rubber meets the road and where many organizations simply go off the road into the weeds. It's easy to get caught up in a myriad of complex details that can derail the production deployment of your high-value analytics. These complexities can be categorized into three major groups:

- People
- Process
- Technology

Although people, process, and technology can derail a project if executed poorly, they can also be enablers to help achieve successful production deployment if implemented well.

We've spent quite a bit of time on technology and won't belabor technology in this chapter. Instead in this chapter, we dive into topics that haven't been covered in previous chapters. We touched on some of the processes to establish an analytics roadmap earlier and now turn our attention to how you can create sustainable value creation through your analytics roadmap. We also focus on one of the most unwieldy parts of deploying analytics: people. This discussion includes topics such as how to best attract and retain top analytics talent as well as how to best organize analytics teams for success.

We need a new generation of analytic professionals who think holistically and understand how to apply a wide range of analytic approaches to business issues and problems.

Analytics talent is a scarce resource today, and the organizations seeking to build analytics teams are finding it difficult to identify, attract, and retain analytics talent. In this chapter, we highlight research from Talent Analytics regarding how to attract and retain analytics talent. But to start the discussion, we focus on a discussion of the business culture and environment because, as you'll discover, those with analytics talent are seeking an atmosphere where they can be challenged and contribute to business objectives. People with analytics talent may join an organization, but without the right culture, they will quickly move on to the next opportunity.

Culture

Business culture is defined as the sharing of values and practices by the members of the organization in the enterprise. Businesses with an analytic culture value fact-based decision making and implement this value by embedding analytics throughout their business to take actions that result in valuable business impact.

In large, existing organizations, analytics maturity develops over a period of time from reactive reporting of past results to proactive anticipation of future events first through predictive analytics and then moving toward prescriptive analytics that use sophisticated optimization techniques. Today's business startups often have the advantage of being able to leapfrog existing businesses by using predictive and prescriptive analytics at the outset with powerful recommendation and scoring engines that allow them to level the playing field with industry giants.

The large existing enterprises typically start out measuring current results and establishing goals or key performance indicators (KPIs). They can implement this goal through simple technology, such as spreadsheets, or through more sophisticated scorecards and then dashboard that business intelligence to measure the results of past performance. Over time, enterprises start migrating toward predictive analytics where the business anticipates likely future outcomes and takes actions based on that informed viewpoint. Because credibility is established in the predictive analytics, the organization typically starts to embed analytics into business processes that can either automate the decision making or take into account much more complex situations and provide a well-informed set of recommendations to an individual for the final decision among a set of good recommendations.

Whether it is a startup that is comfortable and leverages analytics from the start or whether it is a large, existing enterprise that is moving up the analytics maturity curve, common attributes in the culture allow analytics to thrive and serve as a magnet to attract analytic talent. These businesses have a culture that embraces, fosters, and cultivates

- Curiosity
- Problem solving
- Experimentation
- Change
- Evidence

Curiosity

"We keep moving forward, opening new doors, and doing new things, because we're curious and curiosity keeps leading us down new paths."

—Walt Disney

Curiosity seekers are people who are inquisitive, love learning, and are continually improving. Organizations that foster curiosity allow people to connect the dots both internally between various processes as well as with customers and suppliers. Curiosity combined with problem solving is a powerful combination that allows cross-functional teams to collaborate, sharing their domain expertise to identify and resolve business issues or exploit windows of opportunity to drive new value for the business. Fostering curiosity gives the organization permission to experiment and try new ideas. An organization steeped in curiosity and experimenting leads to thinking outside the box that can lead to disruptive innovation and significant business value. Thinking outside the box means asking questions, challenging assumptions, tolerating contrarian views, and accepting nonlinear thinking. This also means the organization has to tolerate failure because experimentation won't always result in immediate productive gains for the enterprise. However, the lessons learned from the failed experimentation should be shared to ingrain the lessons for the experimenters and the broader team. Through the use of a disciplined, objective, closed loop process to debrief experiments—successful and failed—the collective wisdom of the broader organization can be improved for future experiments. Debriefing also aids in developing the storytelling ability of the organization. Storytelling is key to socializing analytics in a way that is contextual and meaningful in the organization. Through storytelling, the problem is clearly identified and the transferrable lesson with evidence is clearly spelled out for the audience. Drawing analogies to other industries is another way for organizations to brainstorm, learn, and adapt transferrable lessons by applying analytic approaches used in other domains to the situations in your industry.

Problem Solving

"If I had an hour to solve a problem, I'd spend 55 minutes thinking about the problem and 5 minutes thinking about solutions."

—Albert Einstein

Problem solvers seek to achieve a goal by identifying issues, bottlenecks, and constraints and then creating a solution that will allow the organization to achieve the goal. Problem-solving organizations often promote problem solving as a means to creating operational efficiency, high performance, and relentless execution. Problem-solving organizations look beyond the symptoms to identify root causes of issues, problems, and bottlenecks and then seek to resolve or minimize with a solution. This often requires good collaboration and communication between various groups in a business to resolve issues. Problem-solving organizations seek to continually improve.

Experimentation

"I have not failed. I've just found 10,000 ways that won't work."

—Thomas Edison

Organizations that seek to break new ground test out new innovative ideas, which means they must tolerate failure, because not every new idea will result in success. Learning from mistakes and failures is critical to evolve potential solutions. An organization that promotes experimentation seeks out creative and scientific types who think outside the box and embrace nonlinear and contrarian thinking. Edward de Bono identified a process for organizational creative thinking in his landmark book *Six Thinking Hats*,[1] including "green hat thinking"—which is de Bono's symbol for creative thinking. During the "green hat thinking," individuals generate provocative, challenging, and inflammatory statements as a method to inspire new ideas. Ingenuity is a hallmark trait of organizations that use techniques such as these to generate clever and inventive new ideas and solutions.

---

[1] Edward de Bono, *Six Thinking Hats* (New York: Back Bay Books, 1999).

Change

"The secret of change is to focus all of your energy, not on fighting the old, but on building the new."

—Socrates

At no time in history has business been conducted as fluidly as it is today. This is a result of ongoing tectonic shifts in macroeconomic factors that have made our world competitive on an unrivaled, global scale. The only constant is that change will continue to be constant and that businesses have to institutionalize agility to adapt to the ever-changing world around them. This means that organizations must move from rigid, hierarchical organizations to more organic, self-organizing organizations that embrace and capitalize on change. Although leading innovator organizations often pride themselves on adapting to market shifts, there are self-reflecting organizations that bide their time and capitalize on change by employing fast follower execution strategies. Change doesn't imply being first; however, it does imply evolving to the changing landscape that aligns with the overall business strategy and keeps the organization current and relevant in the marketplace.

Evidence

"Facts are stubborn things; and whatever may be our wishes, our inclinations, or the dictates of our passions, they cannot alter the state of facts and evidence."

—John Adams

Evidence or fact-based decision-making organizations are relentless in collecting and analyzing data to make business decisions. This does not mean collecting exhaustive data before making decisions; it simply means using the best available data to make the best decision as quickly as possible and then continue to learn and improve with new data.

These same organizations often overlook the need to train everyone in the organization on analytics so they understand how to synthesize and trust the data to make decisions at all levels in the organization. This training should awaken the organization to the possibilities of how data can be used rather than focusing on a particular software tool. This helps the organization identify the ways that analytics can be used to help propel the business forward. Those organizations that are successful in using data to make decisions train their organizations on two fronts: (1) how to frame the right business questions to use data to get the answers and (2) how to use software tools to get the answers.

Data Scientist Role

Although the term *data scientist* was coined in 1960, it wasn't until the term *Big Data* hit the market in 2011 that the term became prevalent and companies started aggressively seeking the allusive data scientist. The reality is that modern analytics talent falls into many disciplines, experiences, and skills; and organizations are starting to realize that the ideal triumvirate of computer science, math, and domain expertise is extremely difficult to find in any individual. Finding individuals with deep computer science skills in multiple software languages, various software tools, and a thorough grasp of software design is difficult in itself. Never mind when those skills are coupled with deep knowledge of applied math, statistics, and operations research. This is the reason businesses often forgo the most important attribute of functional or industry domain expertise and business savvy. This realization is causing organizations to evolve and mature analytic role definitions in organizations.

Quantitative research about data scientists is just starting to make its way into the public. This research includes information about the skills, experience, education, and qualitative characteristics of data scientists. Leading studies by Talent Analytics[2] conducted in 2012 and 2013 show the "fingerprint" for a variety of analytic professionals based on raw talent characteristics. Such raw talent includes criteria such as curiosity, risk taking, and value-based criteria such as "do things the right way."

According to Greta Roberts, founder and CEO of Talent Analytics, "With analytic professionals, now we know what kind of fingerprint data scientists possess. This allows an organization to seek out internal candidates in other areas of the business that have the data scientist fingerprint. Instead of simply seeking a particular skill, such as the analytic programming language R, they identify super-curious people. Super-curious people love to learn, and they can teach themselves. By using a raw talent fingerprint, it actually expands the talent network and expands the areas of places where they can go and look for analytic talent."

The studies include results supported by the popular press and industry hype but also include surprising results. According to the Talent Analytics study, data scientists are largely young (57% under 40) and overwhelmingly male (72%). The gender trend remains similar across all age groups. In terms of education, the study found fewer doctorates than hypothesized—only 16%. Almost half of the analytics professionals surveyed (47%) had master's degrees, and the remainder (36%) had bachelor's degrees. The areas of study were as expected, dominated by math, statistics, and business. Only five subjects had "creative degrees" in music or other arts. Although educational degrees often fail to highlight creative mindsets, the study

---

[2] See "Benchmarking Analytical Talent," December 2012, http://www. talentanalytics.com/talent-analytics-corp/research-study/, and "Four Functional Clusters of Analytics Professionals," July 2013.

showed that 54% of respondents had a very high creative raw talent score.

The talent fingerprint is also crucial in recruiting analytic talent because it identifies the underlying drivers for analytic talent. The data from both Rexer[3] and Talent Analytics studies show that analytic talent want to work on complex, challenging projects that provide their organization with meaningful impact. Roberts shared this information with a large consulting firm that was having problems attracting analytic talent, and the firm wholeheartedly agreed. Roberts was telling the consultancy, "We work with three or four recruiting firms, and everybody says that the reason that they're not attracting analytics professionals and that they are saying 'no' to offers is because of money. However, that is not what the data shows. The data shows that analytics professionals don't care about money; they care about solving interesting and complex problems. They care about continuing to be valued for their curiosity and their ability to learn." The hiring manager from the consultancy went on to state, "That is so weird that you said that. Our team keeps saying it is because of money, but I've had this little itch that says that is not what it is, because we keep offering analytic professionals a 30-percent uplift on their current salaries, and they're not coming here." In fact, analytic professionals often cite the reason for leaving a company is that they are bored and they are leaving to go to another company where they can learn more. This was supported in the Talent Analytics study that showed that data scientists value mental stimulation over monetary incentives (see Exhibit 11.1).

Although analytic professionals value salary, they also respond well to other typical research and scientific incentives such as additional training, time off to work on interesting work, time to contribute to open source projects, and opportunities to publish or speak publicly about their work. Roberts has also vetted this out in her work:

[3] Rexer Analytics, "2013 Data Miner Survey," http://www.rexeranalytics.com/Data-Miner-Survey-Results-2013.html.

"Who is going to turn down great money? Nobody is. You know, the economy is bad. But analytic professionals often make the move to a new company, they take the money, they get into that role, and then they're put in a data preparation role—forever. And they get bored and they leave. They go somewhere else where they can learn more. Using data, we can objectively measure and identify other criteria to increase retention. We've learned that you can offer things to people like training or time off, or things that really are meaningful to them." The 2013 Data Miner Survey by Rexer Analytics also showed that greater appreciation and autonomy while working on analytic projects was the most significant factor in keeping analytic professionals satisfied with their job. Other key factors include interesting projects and educational opportunities, which correspond with the Talent Analytics finding that analytic professional are curious, active learners.

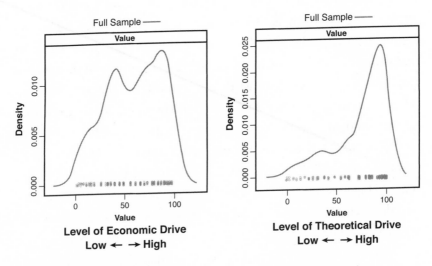

Exhibit 11.1　Evidence That Data Scientists Value Mental Stimulation over Wallet Stimulation

Further evaluation of the Talent Analytics survey in 2012 showed that analytic talent clustered into four analytic roles: (1) Generalists, (2) Data Preparation, (3) Programmers, and (4) Managers. These roles were based on time spent on the following typical analytic tasks (see Exhibit 11.2):

- Analysis design
- Data acquisition
- Data preparation
- Analysis
- Data mining
- Visualization

- Programming
- Interpretation
- Presentation
- Administration
- Management

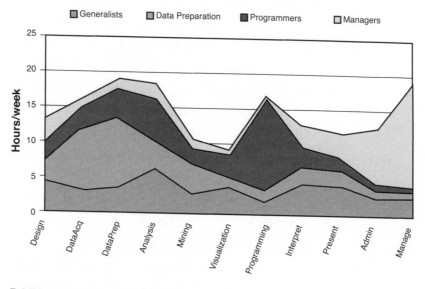

Time Spent in Analytics Pipeline, by Functional Cluster

Exhibit 11.2   Time Spent in Analytic Pipeline Stage

The study also measured business-relevant personality traits—four specific behavioral factors and seven specific ambition factors. The ambition factors measure personal drivers. Ambition factors drive people to roles, business cultures, and situations they find particularly compelling. Ambitions, as measured by Talent Analytics, remain constant regardless of additional skills or experience. Ambitions are robust across an individual's lifetime and can be used to correlate innate human characteristics to top performance such as metrics that show top-performing sales reps tend to be driven by money or power, among other characteristics. When correlations are found between innate human characteristics and job performance, employers can use this information to seek out candidates with these characteristics when hiring.

The Talent Analytics study results revealed an undeniable "raw talent fingerprint" for data scientists. Here are some highlights:

- Data scientists have a cognitive "attitude" and will search for deeper knowledge about everything.

- They are driven to be creative and will want to create not only solutions, but also elegant solutions (that is, the code could be more elegant, or there might be a better graph to visualize the solution). They will thrive in an organizational culture that values different approaches and out-of-the-box thinking.

- Data scientists have a strong desire to "do things the right way" and will encourage others to do the same. They will be comfortable speaking to defend what they believe to be right, even in the face of controversy.

- They have an extremely high sense of quality, standards, and detail orientation, often evaluating others by these same traits. They are highly conscientious and will provide careful follow-through on detailed projects and complex assignments.

- Data scientists tend to be somewhat restrained and reticent in showing emotions and may be less verbal at team or organizational meetings unless asked for input or if the topic is one of high importance.

- Data scientists may take calculated, educated risks—only after a thoughtful analysis of facts, data, and potential outcomes. They persuade others on the team by careful attention to detail and through facts, data, and logic, not emotion. Data scientists appreciate security in projects, systems, and job culture.

One of the key findings of the Talent Analytics study was that the role of data scientist is just too broad for practical hiring. Just like the role of "doctor" is descriptive but inadequate to describe the various competencies under that broad label, a data scientist has specialties. After all, how many doctors exist who are heart surgeons, dermatologists, podiatrists, and neurologists all in one person?

Categories and subcategories that come under the data scientist label help define the specific role, specialty, and subsequent tasks. We suggest leaders and hiring managers not confuse the job family of data scientist with the job title or role description. As managers break the analytics workflow into specific roles and tasks, requirements will become more focused and the qualified talent pool will expand.

Two strong characteristics stand out across all four analytic roles (see Exhibit 11.3):

- Very strong intellectual curiosity (theoretical drive)
- Strong drive to create out-of-the-box solutions (creative drive)

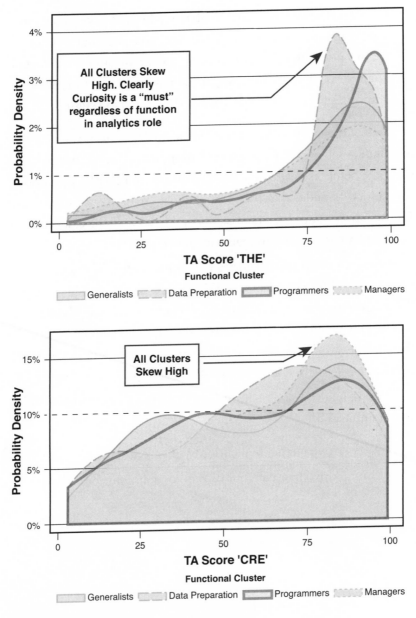

Exhibit 11.3 Key Drivers for Data Scientists

Data Prep Professionals

Each cluster of analytic roles varies a bit. Analytics professionals who specialize in data prep spend a majority (46%) of their time on data acquisition and data prep activities (see Exhibit 11.4). Analytics professionals in this cluster, as with all the other clusters, spend times across many activities; their secondary activities (analytics, data mining, design, interpretation, and presentation) are closely related to the data prep activity. Data prep analysts are different from other analytic roles in that they are decidedly less competitive (less politically motivated). They are not interested in upward mobility and don't view that as a reward. Data prep professionals demonstrate the highest aptitude for detail and are least likely to make mistakes.

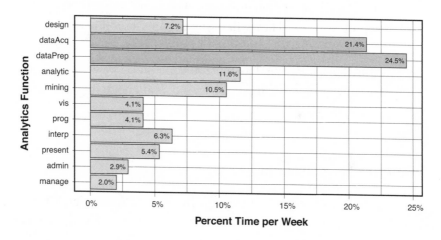

Exhibit 11.4   Time Spent by Data Prep Analytics Professionals

- **Sourcing**—Data preparation candidates are likely to be found in other areas of your organization, particularly roles that are detail rich. Remember that aptitude for detail and accuracy needs to be reviewed in addition to a requirement for strong intellectual curiosity and creativity. Of course, it is vital to evaluate intelligence and training for such a role, but data preparation requires the least statistical domain knowledge out of the four clusters.

- **Hiring**—In trying to incentivize candidates to this role, do not focus on political growth, career advancement, or a future with lots of senior-level visibility.

- **Managing**—Data preparation staff will want details about their goals and performance versus general comments. They will keep details on their own projects and performance and be disappointed if this is not similarly tracked.

- **Retaining**—The work in the data preparation cluster is definitely on the back-office side of analytics, but it is a large and essential function. Professionals in this role share much of the creativity, intellectual interests, and beliefs as other analytics professionals. They will easily become bored and leave for another role that satisfies their intellectual curiosity more fully. Ultimately, they are looking for a mentally challenging role that appeals to their natural curiosity and creativity more than career advancement.

Analytics Programmers

Analytics professionals who specialize in analytical programming spend a majority (33%) of their time writing computer code to manipulate and process data (see Exhibit 11.5). They spend more than three times the time programming than any other analytic professional. Similar to other analytic professionals, they divide their workday among a wide variety of other analytics-related activities with an emphasis on closely related activities such as analytics, data prep, and data acquisition. The Talent Analytics study showed this is the youngest age group (almost half under 29 years old) and least experienced (over half have less than 5 years of experience). This group also lacked the desire to climb the corporate ladder. From an aptitude perspective, analytics programmers have the strongest desire to collaborate, making sure they gain alignment on their work.

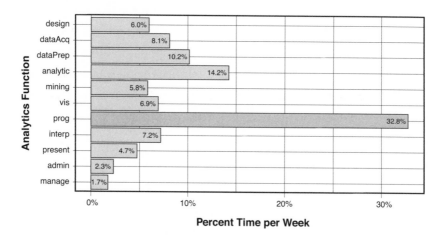

Exhibit 11.5   Time Spent by Analytics Programmers

- **Sourcing**—Look for analytics programmers inside your organization in current programming roles. Make note of those who installed beta versions of software, who push the limits of functionality, or who constantly experiment. Recent college graduates could be a good source; ask what projects they're working on even if just for their own personal projects.

- **Hiring**—Candidates in this role are most interested in learning new software, staying on the leading edge of technology and analytics, being given some free rein to experiment and explore and be involved in continuous learning. The further away they get from doing hands-on work, the more bored and dissatisfied they will get.

- **Managing**—Given the age and experience level of analytics programmers, managers would be wise to take the time to mentor them about general business knowledge, business expectations, and perhaps how to maneuver politically inside an organization. Their lack of political savvy could land them in trouble if not given some insight and boundaries. They will be quick studies and will be happy to learn.

- **Retaining**—Like all analytics professionals, this cluster will easily become bored. Financial incentives and promises that they will move up the ladder will not appeal to them nor make them feel valued or challenged. Ultimately, they are looking for a mentally challenging role that appeals to their natural curiosity and creativity more than career advancement.

Analytics Managers

Analytics managers spend a majority (57%) of their time managing their analytics team and performing a variety of administrative tasks (see Exhibit 11.6). Their workload leans toward managing direct reports and projects and then presenting results of projects to their customers.

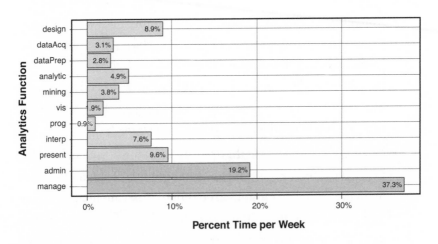

Exhibit 11.6   Time Spent by Analytics Managers

Analytics managers are older (less than 10% were under 29 in the research) and have broader experience. In the research, managers had a strong competitive and political aptitude that stood out from the other analytic professional clusters. Managers also had a higher altruistic score, signaling a drive to mentor and help their team.

- **Sourcing**—Management candidates can be located from existing analytics professionals or other management areas inside the organization. They will be easy to identify because they will be very focused (even from the point of being a candidate) on what they need to do to advance and move up the management chain.

- **Hiring**—Management candidates will be focused on advancing and one day managing their own team of direct reports. If advancement is a real opportunity, this would be something to point out in a job posting, job description, or interview. But know, if they come on board, they will not forget that they were told they could advance and will feel robbed if this opportunity isn't addressed.

- **Managing**—Those with management aspirations will feel less motivated until their path for advancement is clear. They will see leadership and visibility to other leaders as a bonus and something to strive for. Given that they have less of a focus on results, perhaps their advancement could be tied to goal achievement and completing projects on time.

- **Retaining**—Managers in the Talent Analytics study showed that what they care most about is learning, not being bored, and being able to advance inside the organization. Ironically, the sample of managers were least interested in financial rewards. So, as with other types of analytics professionals, they won't turn down additional money, but it won't be a factor in retaining them in a job they don't enjoy.

Recent research published by O'Reilly[4] validates that data scientists have quite a diverse set of skills, including statistics, machine

---

[4] Harlan D. Harris, Sean Patrick Murphy, and Marck Vaisman, *Analyzing the Analyzers*, O'Reilly Media, 2013, http://cdn.oreillystatic.com/oreilly/radarreport/0636920029014/Analyzing_the_Analyzers.pdf.

learning, databases, operations research, business intelligence (BI), social or physical sciences, and more. This has led to a misalignment of expectations by hiring organizations and managers that seek the "perfect" candidate with deep expertise in many, if not all, of these skills plus strong communication and leadership capabilities. The disconnect between the ideal data scientist and reality has led to the notion that there is a huge shortage of data scientists in the market. To help companies come to grips with the hype, human resource teams are seeking out expertise from knowledgeable in-house experts to define multiple, more realistic job descriptions for data scientists. Through this collaboration, companies are evolving their job descriptions to be better aligned with resources in the market. This realignment of expectations is leading to a better pipeline of qualified candidates, better job satisfaction, and bottom-line results for organizations.

Analytics Generalists

Analytics generalists, found in both small and very large organizations, don't spend a majority of time on any focused area (see Exhibit 11.7). Analytics generalists appear to be a hybrid of the "raw talent" traits contained in the other three analytics professionals. These seasoned experts could be described as most like analytics managers with less inclination to be political or controlling, and more inclination for tangible results while tending toward doing careful and detailed work.

Sample Analytics Job Family Structure

Let's consider a sample mature software company with multiple billions in revenue that has decided to infuse analytics throughout its business and software. This company created a job family for data science in recognition that there isn't just one type of data scientist but instead there are multiple types needed for a team. In the data science job family, the company established two tracks:

- Individual contributor
- People manager

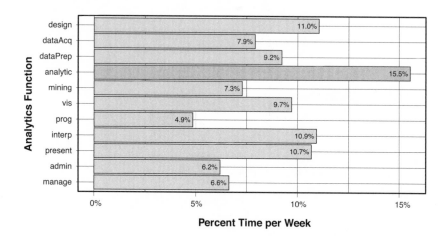

Exhibit 11.7   Time Spent by Analytics Generalists

Next, it defined multiple levels to accommodate job functions from entry level to very seasoned professionals (see Exhibit 11.8). This allowed the company to designate folks from just out of school all the way through best-in-class analytics professionals.

With each level, the company identified multiple skills categories and a range of expertise expected for each level (see Exhibits 11.9 and 11.10). The skills categories included the following:

- Quantitative and technical
- Business knowledge and solution design
- Influence
- People leadership

Exhibit 11.8 Sample Data Science Job Family Titles

Level					
Track	**Entry**	**Professional**	**Expert**	**Senior**	**Leader**
Individual Contributor	Data Scientist	Senior Data Scientist	Principal Data Scientist	Distinguished Data Scientist	Data Scientist Fellow
People Leader		Manager Data Science	Director Data Science	VP Data Science	SVP Data Science

Skill Group \ Title	Data Scientist	Sr. Data Scientist	Principal Data Scientist	Distinguished Data Scientist	Data Scientist Fellow
Quantitative and technical	◑	◑	◕	◕	●
Business knowledge and solution design	◔	◑	◑	◕	●
Influence	◔	◑	◑	◕	◕
People leadership	◔	◔	◑	◑	◕

Exhibit 11.9   Sample Data Science Individual Track Definitions

Skill Group \ Title	Manager Data Science	Director Data Science	VP Data Science	SVP Data Science
Quantitative and technical	◑	◕	●	●
Business knowledge and solution design	◑	◕	●	●
Influence	◑	◕	◕	●
People leadership	◑	◕	◕	●

Exhibit 11.10   Sample Data Science Manager Track Definitions

For each of the skill categories, the company defined specific skills and minimal expectations (see Exhibit 11.11). For example, in the quantitative and technical category the skills are defined as:

- Data extraction, cleansing, and transformation
- Basic analytics
- Intermediate analytics
- Advanced analytics
- Analytical software tools
- Software design and development

If this company had a clearly defined analytics roadmap segmented into strategic, managerial, and execution applications, it would be simple to associate roles to support each of the segments. On one hand, to support strategic applications, the organization would need motivated, concise communicators to collaborate with executives or the C-suite to understand the business issues and problems. On the other hand, you need to hire analytic professionals with domain expertise to quickly get to the answers for managerial applications. For execution applications, you need developers with integration experience to embed analytics into existing applications.

Although the job titles, skills categories, and required skills in this example are fairly universal, each organization should create its own definitions that are tailored to the needs of the organization. For example, some organizations may need to place an emphasis on spatial analytic skills or operations research, whereas others may not need these specialized skills at all.

After this software company had clear and agreed-upon role definitions for data scientists with the minimal skills and scope of responsibilities defined, the company assessed the gap in the current analytic teams to achieve its business objectives. This approach has allowed the company to create an effective hiring and training plan. Being able to attract and retain analytic talent is easier when there is a clearly defined career path and meaningful incentives for both technical and managerial analytic professionals.

Skill Group \ Title				
Data extraction, cleansing, transformation	Skilled with SQL and relational databases	Knowledgeable in advanced data retrieval tools	Proficient on retrieving, cleansing and integrating data from multiple source systems	Expert knowledge and experience with distributed databases and tools
Basic analytics	Skilled with descriptive statistics	Knowledgeable and experienced with basic visualization techniques	Experienced with experimental design and hypothesis testing	Expert knowledge and experience with predictive analytics using various forms of regression
Intermediate analytics	Skills with advanced visualization techniques	Proficient with predictive modeling using decision trees	Proficient with feature selection and dimensionality reduction	Expert knowledge and experience with time series analysis
Advanced analytics	Skilled in both supervised and unsupervised machine learning	Experienced with text analytics	Proficient with analysis of network data	Experience and knowledge with creating proprietary algorithms when necessary and/or applying simulation and optimization
Analytical software tools	Skilled with multiple analytic tools	Experienced with developing analytic tools that are used by data science team	Proficient with deploying in analytic tools for business stakeholders	Expert and experienced with embedding analytics into operational systems
Software design and development	Skilled in multiple programming languages	Experienced building effective prototypes and POCs (proof of concept)	Applies best software development best practices	Expert and experienced with designing, coding, testing, deploying and maintaining analytic software

Exhibit 11.11   Sample Quantitative and Technical Skill Category Definitions

Finding Data Scientists

You've likely heard the expression, "birds of a feather flock together," and this is certainly true for analytic professionals. As identified earlier, internal candidates can be identified based on success criteria identified in the raw talent fingerprint. Additionally, top talent seek external peer recognition and often present at industry conferences such as Strata, KDD, INFORMS, Developer Week, and many other industry and vendor conferences. These forums provide an excellent venue for recruiting top talent. Use this venue to showcase the types of problems you are seeking to solve because this is a natural magnet for talent. Another venue for seeking top talent is in analytic competitions such as KDD Cup and crowd source venues such as Kaggle. Lastly, analytics professional industry groups such as data mining (KDD), statistics (JSM), operations research (INFORMS, GECCO), user groups (R, SAS), and open source projects (Julia, R, Spark, SciPy, Rapid Miner, KNIME, Orange, Weka, and so on) provide a terrific venue for identifying top talent. Don't forget to ask your current analytics talent where they go and what they follow. This information will provide additional insights into ideal venues for recruiting analytic talent.

Attracting Data Scientists

The most effective way to entice data scientists to apply for your open position is to interest them in the analytical work they'll be doing. They are curious people and will want their curiosity fed, so intrigue them with project details in your job postings and conversations.

Most job ads are designed to exclude candidates. The research by Talent Analytics shows that data scientists are very concerned with overcommitting. "Requirements" are often seen as absolutes. Because most data scientists enjoy learning on their own—a "requirement" for a particular skill (for example, R or SAS or other easily learnable technical expertise) may exclude otherwise fantastic candidates. A good alternative would be to leave these "excluding" items out of the ad and ask such questions in the interview.

The Talent Analytics study shows data scientists strongly tend toward being thoughtful, careful, and specific in their answers. They are listeners, not talkers. Some in the interview process could judge this trait negatively if they are looking for a charismatic conversationalist. The innate capacity to happily wrestle with data tends to be opposite to the innate capacity of charming people during an interview.

To determine candidates' curiosity propensity, observe whether these data scientist candidates ask a lot of questions. They are natural researchers and have done their homework; they will want specifics and may get frustrated without answers. If candidates show up unprepared and without many questions, that could signal a lack of curiosity, which could be a barrier to success in this role.

As highlighted in the Talent Analytics research, scientists are incentivized differently than salespeople, lawyers, and many other professions. Although salespeople crave financial rewards, scientists crave peer recognition as vetted out by the late Gerry DeSanctis in her research. Be sure to provide opportunities for data scientists to share their knowledge with other teams—both internally and externally. Allow data scientists to present their innovations and research at industry conferences and to publish their work in peer and industry journals. Be sure to highlight and recognize their contributions to the success of the organization. These incentives, along with challenging and interesting problems to solve, are the keys to retaining top analytic talent.

As we've discovered, a culture that welcomes, promotes, and rewards curiosity, problem solving, experimentation, change, and evidence-based decision making serves as a natural magnet for attracting analytics talent. Understanding the raw talent fingerprint of data scientists and their roles—as generalists, data preparation, programmers, and managers—permits an organization to establish an appropriate family of analytic professional career paths.

Summary

Although analytics talent is scarce today, there are opportunities to leverage existing resources if jobs are divided into roles that align with the analytics workflow employed by your organization. Building or moving to a fact-based culture serves as a natural magnet for attracting and retaining top analytics talent. Remember that analytics teams want to make a contribution to the business objectives. Be sure to celebrate and reward successful contributions by analytics talent so they know their work is valuable and their contributions are important to the business. In the next chapter, we'll discuss how to effectively organize analytic talent.

12

Organizing Analytics Teams

Overview

Determining how to most effectively organize your analytics team involves several considerations. As with any other organizational structure, the team's organization can change over time based on business goals, changing business requirements, and the analytics adoption within the organization.

Centralized versus Decentralized Analytics Team

Creating the right organizational structure for your analytics talent is key to the ongoing success, impact, and retention of your analytics team. The organizational structure will change over time as the team and business grow and change. But one of the first considerations is whether to centralize or decentralize the analytics team.

Centralizing the team allows analytics professionals to share common best practices that leverage the experience and expertise of the team (see Exhibit 12.1). This is often a way to start analytics teams, even if long term the team will be decentralized, because it allows the team to develop a uniform foundation for performing analysis. Centralized teams usually develop common methods, processes, practices, and tools for developing and deploying analytic models. However, centralized teams are typically disconnected from the business, and analytics are driven from a top-down approach. Although this approach may seem out of touch with the business, it often is a way to introduce strategic analytics into the organization or to adapt analytic approaches from other industries and use cases for the business.

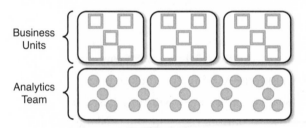

Business Units

Analytics Team

Pros and Cons
- Leverage best practices
- Disconnected from business
- Top-down analytics
- Focus on strategic analytics

Exhibit 12.1   Centralized Analytics Team

Decentralized teams are collocated with lines of business and tend to develop a deeper level of understanding of the business (see Exhibit 12.2). Traditionally, quants and statisticians in banks are decentralized and are part of the market risk, trading, or marketing functions. Although this organizational structure aligns the analytics team with the business objectives, it tends to drive reactionary behavior that focuses on business execution rather than proactive behavior that leads the organization to achieve strategic business objectives. Decentralized teams typically have inconsistent practices and processes that result in redundant efforts and problems with integrating work products. This leads to inconsistent results from different teams. In turn, this causes confusion and additional work to synchronize answers from various teams.

Business Units with Analysts {

Pros and Cons
• Deeper business knowledge
• Aligned with business
• Reactive
• Inconsistent practices and processes
• Focus on strategic analytics

Exhibit 12.2   Decentralized Analytics Team

Hybrid approaches combine the centralized and decentralized structures to balance business alignment with efficient utilization of scarce analytic resources (see Exhibit 12.3). Typically, the team is centralized for administrative tasks such as for establishing and sharing best practices, training, and mentoring. The hybrid approach uses a decentralized model to collocate analytics professionals with the business for alignment and to develop a deeper understanding of the business. As the analytic and line of business professionals work side by side, they each develop a better understanding of the business and the analytics. Because the line of business professional is intimately involved in defining the analytics for the business, this person understands the results as they evolve over time, and the line of business professional develops trust and credibility in the results of the analytics professionals and their work product. Establishing credibility early is key to the organization gaining momentum on building and deploying analytics throughout the organization.

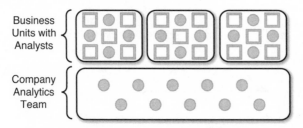

Pros and Cons
- Deeper business knowledge
- Aligned with business
- Reactive
- Consistent practices and processes
- Focus on strategic analytics

Exhibit 12.3 Hybrid Analytics Team

Let's consider a real-world example of an analytics organization that has evolved quickly over the past few years. George Roumeliotis was one of the first data scientists at Intuit back in 2008. He saw the team grow and the adoption of analytics become more strategic over the past few years. According to Roumeliotis:

Transformative is what we want to achieve. We all want to have massive impacts. However, in my experience, you can't [go] from no use of analytics to using analytics to create transformational change. I think you've got to go through some intermediate steps where you are showing tangible value. You start off with smaller scale successes to demonstrate value to the business leaders. I just don't think you can skip over that. Believe me, I've tried. It just doesn't work for me in an established company at least. I don't think you can go from no use of analytics to dramatically impactful things without some intermediate steps.

At Intuit, I was one of the first data scientists here, six years ago, and back then the work was all about marketing, basically, marketing optimization. I engaged with the marketing leaders and I had a number of successes around marketing optimization, and then it's almost like an evolutionary process. Then two years ago, I started pitching to business leaders and executing projects around understanding how users behave inside on-line products and understanding where they get hung up and how to use the clickstream, analyze the clickstream to go back and then improve the product. There's less friction in Turbo Tax for example. In two years I went from influencing marketing to influencing product. Now we're making this huge push to create data products, data driven products, and leverage these awesome data assets that we have around us. But it's only because there was credibility built up from the earlier projects.

Although credibility is a working assumption in the decentralized model as analytic professionals and business leaders develop peer relationships, the centralized model in particular needs to develop credibility via successes early:

Having an analytics team in a central group adds a layer of complexity and challenge. In the centralized group we're trying to use data and analytics to do something dramatic, something radical. The central group is challenged to be taken seriously as a real thought partner and strategic partner to business units since we're not part of the business units. There's no perfect answer, because both centralized and decentralized organizational models have their problems. If you're trying to influence from the center or as a consultant, you know if you step into the shoes of the business unit, what are they really thinking when you come along? Are they going to give you something meaningful? Is the product manager going to give you something that's mission critical that could impact them achieving their bonus at the end of the year? Why should they do that, why would they take that risk? What control do they have over you? Are they going to give you something mission critical just because you can execute, first of all[?] Will you be there to maintain in the production systems? There's just a whole range of thoughts that go through the head of a business leader and a business unit, when somebody central or a consultant comes along. This can be overcome but the key is to take a step by step process of building confidence and trust, based on execution.

As Roumeliotis stated, there is no perfect model. Decentralized or distributed analytic teams experience other issues:

> The distributed model has its challenges too. The biggest challenge is that folks, who are embedded analysts, have a tendency to work on "run the business" type of problems. The business, by definition, is putting its energies into execution and if there's innovation going on, that's rather unusual, I think. They're trying to make next quarter's goals, and so the analysts, their focus is, from my experience, all around how do we get that goal? For example, "How do we tune our marketing programs?" to hit the goal.

Center of Excellence

An Analytics Center of Excellence (COE) is another way to create a hybrid organization structure. Some businesses create the COE as virtual or matrixed teams, whereas other businesses create a permanent team of analytic professionals in the COE. The Analytic COE is typically responsible for analytics training and establishing standards.

This team typically has ongoing responsibility for initial and ongoing development of training materials and training sessions for the entire organization. The most successful analytics businesses train everyone on analytic concepts and how analytics can be used to derive value for the business. This includes educating everyone on the analytics roadmap, the business goals, and expectations for each of the analytic projects on the roadmap. When everyone is educated on the roadmap, the entire business team will begin to understand how analytics can be used in their business area to derive business value. With this understanding, everyone can contribute new ideas for how data and analytics can be used to help pose and answer questions to execute better in their segment of the business. Then, as appropriate for the role, the business can train individuals on specific analytic tools and software.

The Analytics COE establishes standards of analysis and measurement. When business units perform analysis independently of one another, there is a risk that reports will show different or conflicting results. There are two reasons for this: Complex business concepts may mean different things to different departments, and departments may have an interest in showing favorable results.

As an example of the first source of variation in measurements, consider the case of measuring customer churn in a Telco. To the operations department, *churn* may mean any closed account because every account closure requires department effort and influences total costs. To the marketing department, however, *churn* may be limited to accounts closed voluntarily by the customer because accounts closed for delinquent payments or for customers moving out of the service area do not reflect a competitive loss. The Analytics COE works to establish standard definitions and terminology across departments to avoid misunderstandings.

"Embedded" analysts are often under organizational pressure to perform analysis in such a way that the sponsoring department looks good. In marketing, for example, program managers may place undue emphasis on metrics that measure effort, such as outbound messages or impressions, and not enough emphasis on metrics that measure the actual impact of their programs. Moreover, program managers often try to claim credit for events whose connection to their program is tenuous; for example, an advertising manager may argue that any observed increase in sales is attributable to advertising placed concurrently with the increased sales. When individual program managers choose the metrics that make their program look good, it is difficult or impossible to compare results across programs and allocate budgets appropriately. The Analytics COE establishes consistent metrics across programs and departments and sponsors the tools and methods required to implement these common metrics.

Chief Data Officer versus Chief Analytics Officer

Just as the role of a data scientist has emerged over the past few years, so have two executive roles: chief data officer and chief analytics officer. Although the titles of these two roles are often bandied about synonymously, they have very different goals.

Often these two executives may have similar backgrounds, but they utilize that background very differently. The chief data officer is primarily responsible for data assets, data infrastructure, and governance of data. That is, the chief data officer is focused on acquiring and managing data assets. The chief analytics officer is primarily responsible for leveraging the data assets into tangible value for an organization by applying analytic methods to the data assets.

Today, there aren't many organizations that have the luxury of both a chief data officer and a chief analytics officer. However, as analytic teams grow and become more strategic in organizations, more emphasis will be placed on these roles. With their deep understanding of both data and analytics, these two executive roles are key to developing and executing on a unique analytics roadmap for the business.

In the early stages of the Modern Analytics age, these two roles are crucial in establishing organizational credibility within the executive team for evidence-based decision making. "The chief analytics officer can form relationships and educate their peers at that level.

It's one of the most helpful things, just to build awareness and education that analytics can be more than a tactical tool... It's not just like finance or some part of operations. It can be a real strategic lever," states Roumeliotis.

As the Modern Analytics age evolves, the chief data officer will focus more on how to leverage data by really understanding the business well enough to understand how to get additional data to actually achieve what the business wants. Innovative business leaders are really geniuses, they're brilliant at connecting dots, and they get information, even if it's anecdotally, from the industry, from watching people in the industry, from competitive news, and from any other place they can. Analytic organizations today tend to use their internal data. Some organizations buy some outside data. However, the Modern Analytics chief analytic officer and data officer will think about and collaborate on the problem. They'll figure out how they can obtain new data or how they can triangulate, even if they can't get the data directly, to solve the problem. They'll think, "How can I get a reasonable first guess at that information, and with whom could I develop a symbiotic relationship to obtain the data I need?" "How can I leapfrog the competition by developing a more comprehensive model that will improve our performance exponentially?" These executives won't be satisfied with the mundane but will push their teams and organizations to achieve excellence through relentless utilization of data and analytics assets.

At Intuit, Roumeliotis continues thinking about the future with analytics:

> It's not necessarily about buying data. There's a whole open
> data movement, which is the government making a lot of dark
> data available publicly, and most people don't even know
> about that, never mind what it is and how to actually use it to
> their benefit. To me, that's what a chief data officer in the next
> sort of generation will do. Find new data sources and how to

leverage them. To me, the first generation of a chief analytics officer is a lot of education, but a chief analytic officer should be the Thomas Edison, like the light bulb, the ideation person for oh, you know, this is how we could apply this technology to help you. This is a person who should be a sounding board for the rest of the executive team. They can come to a chief analytic officer and say my team or some outside person has come up with this crazy idea and it sounds just too radical for me. They would have the wherewithal to be able to vet the idea.

Lab Team

A lab team is typically a "skunk works" or innovation team that has been set up to drive faster analytic innovation and prototypes. A lab team is typically a smaller, dedicated team that experiments with new technology and new potential analytic applications. This team often has direction established by a chief data officer or chief analytics officer. After the business accepts a prototype, the prototype is transitioned to a production analytics team for deployment and ongoing improvement.

Analytic Program Office

An analytics program office is a project office focused on project governance. The analytics program office is responsible for the successful delivery of the project budget and schedule.

Summary

Choose the best organizational structure that will work for now and evolve that structure as your team experiments, learns, and adapts.

13

What Are You Waiting For?
Go Get Started!

The right strategy for using Modern Analytics is to create and execute your unique analytics roadmap. But do you have to wait till you create and prioritize your analytic projects? Absolutely not!

While you're developing your unique analytics roadmap, identify "no-brainers." These are the low-hanging fruit that have clearly identifiable business value and are easy to build out with the existing infrastructure, tools, and people you have on your team. By doing this, you start building credibility with analytics and producing meaningful business impact. Be sure to fold in these quick wins to the closed-loop process so that they aren't orphaned and that you seek continual improvements from these quick wins.

Big Data and open source are the catalysts that started the transformation from an analytics sellers market to an analytics buyers market. The market—you and many other impatient business executives and analytic teams—is demanding an equivalent disruption in the analytics industry. Although the analytic tools and infrastructure are in the midst of this transformation, businesses also need to change so that they can derive huge potential value from analytics. Analytics is ubiquitous and can be applied to *all* areas within your business to help drive significant business value and unprecedented business impact. One of the challenges for tomorrow's leaders is to identify meaningful ways to infuse analytics into their business faster to take their business to the next level.

To achieve this goal, companies need a unique analytics roadmap tailored to their unique business strategy. Starting with the end in mind—to drive new business value and impact—teams can identify and prioritize potential analytics applications that will catapult the business into a more profitable future.

With a longer-term analytics roadmap, your IT team, ideally led by a chief analytics officer and chief data officer, can design and architect an analytics ecosystem that aligns with your analytics roadmap. Think of the analytics infrastructure as your toolbox to help you build your brighter future. There are many different hammers, but if you know you're doing demolition work, you use a sledgehammer, and if you're doing finish carpentry, you use trim and finish hammers. Use the right infrastructure and tools to fit your unique analytics roadmap.

When you embark on this journey, commit to training your entire team. If your team members clearly understand the goals, they need the right understanding of analytics to help them effectively contribute to the goals. This will help create a common language for everyone on the team—front line personnel, analysts and data scientists, and back-office personnel—to use when discussing analytics. This will institutionalize an analytics culture—a commitment to fact-based decision making—that will permeate and drive the entire organization. This will have the side benefit of making it easier to attract and retain top analytic talent. Remember that analytics is about trial and error. Experimenting is the fuel for creative thinking and innovation in an organization. Develop new ideas, mindsets, and approaches. Adapt analogies from other industries. Extrapolate on old ideas. Identify bottlenecks and seek to eradicate them. By pushing the boundaries and applying analytics to many problems, issues, and opportunities, you can accelerate your learning and drive your business to new heights.

The five types of analytic applications are as follows:

1. Strategic analytics
2. Managerial analytics
3. Operational analytics
4. Scientific analytics
5. Customer-facing analytics

To build your unique analytics roadmap, follow these steps, which were outlined previously:

Step 1   Identify key business objectives.

Step 2   Define your value chain.

Step 3   Brainstorm analytic solution opportunities.

Step 4   Describe analytic solution opportunities.

Step 5   Create decision model.

Step 6   Evaluate analytic solution opportunities.

Step 7   Establish analytics roadmap.

Step 8   Evolve your analytics roadmap.

When you have an analytics roadmap, use the right tools for the right job. For each project, set a goal and then be relentless in meeting or exceeding the goal. After you achieve your goal, take time to celebrate your success. Then go back and learn more to help you continuously improve your results.

Index

A

Abbott, Dean, 26
   case study, 45-50, 52
accuracy of classification, 143
ACID (Atomic, Consistent, Isolation, Durability), 189
ad hoc analysis, 12, 90-91
Adams, John, 210
agent-based modeling, 51
aggregate functions, 166
Air Liquide case study, 43-45, 52
Akaike information criterion (AIC), 146
algorithms in analytics roadmap, 27
Alpine, 168, 178
Alteryx, 167-168
ambition factors of data scientists, 215-216
analysis data set
   building, 133-139
      assembling data, 134
      evaluating data, 134-135
      investigating outliers, 135-136
      missing data, 138-139
      table operations, 137-138
      transforming data, 136-137
   partitioning, 140-141
analytic applications in customer-facing analytics, 102-103
analytic libraries (SQL), 192
analytic personas, 14-15

analytic solutions
   brainstorming, 60-65
   describing, 66-70
   establishing roadmap, 82
   prioritizing, 70-72
   scoring, 73-81
analytic talent. *See* data scientists
analytics
   business culture and, 206-207
      change, 210
      curiosity, 207-208
      evidence, 210-211
      experimentation, 209
      problem solving, 208-209
   business user tools
      Alpine, 168
      Alteryx, 167-168
      IBM SPSS Modeler, 168-169
      RapidMiner, 169
      SAS Enterprise Guide, 170
      SAS Enterprise Miner, 170-171
      Statistica, 171
      usage by user personas, 171
   complexities of deployment, 205
   customer-facing analytics, 62, 100-103
      analytic applications, 102-103
      consumer analytics, 103
      prediction services, 101-102
   descriptive analytics, 62-63
   managerial analytics, 61, 94-96
   operational analytics, 61-62, 96-99